THE COUNTRY DIARY of

GARDEN LORE

JULIA JONES
AND
BARBARA DEER

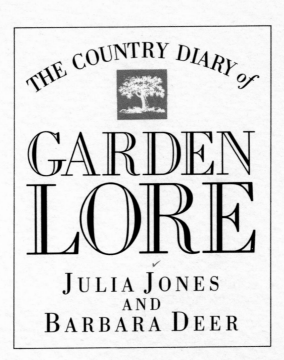

THE COUNTRY DIARY of

GARDEN LORE

JULIA JONES
AND
BARBARA DEER

McGRAW-HILL RYERSON
Toronto · Montreal

For Brian and for Mum and Dad

7633

EDITOR Gwen Edmonds
DESIGNED BY Mathewson Bull
PHOTOGRAPHY Andreas Einsiedel

First published in Great Britain in 1989 by
DORLING KINDERSLEY LIMITED
9 Henrietta Street, London WC2E 8PS

Published in Canada by
McGraw-Hill Ryerson Limited
330 Progress Avenue
Scarborough, Ontario
M1P 2Z5

TYPESET BY Tradespools Ltd, Frome
COLOUR REPRODUCTION by Colourscan, Singapore
PRINTED in Italy by A. Mondadori Editore, Verona

CANADIAN CATALOGUING IN PUBLICATION DATA

Jones, Julia, 1945–
    Calendar of garden lore

Includes bibliographical references.
ISBN 0–07–551055–3

1. Botany – Great Britain – Folklore.
2. Plants – Folklore.   I. Deer, Barbara.   II. Title.

GR780.J66 1990   398′.368′0941   C90–093458–1

Contents

PREFACE

From generation to generation the garden has provided rich and poor alike with food for the family, medicinal herbs and flowers to sweeten the home. The importance of the garden in the lives of our ancestors has made it a place rich in tradition and superstition but it has also given rise to a great store of practical wisdom relating to the general care of the garden and its plants.

Favourite garden plants all had their special qualities – rosemary would cure drunkenness, borage would give courage and happiness to those that ate it. In fact all of the natural world was invested with significance, the shape of a leaf, the cry of a bird, might offer the promise of wealth or marriage or might presage some disaster.

With the absence of weather forecasts the gardener learnt to watch for signs around him, he would observe animals, insects and plants in order to plan his gardening days. A spider tightening his web meant rain was on it way; a large crop of autumn berries a cold winter, but if onion skins were thin then the winter would be mild. These signs are still around us we just need to learn what to look for.

We hope that you will find this calendar of garden lore interesting, informative and amusing with the insight that it gives into the traditional gardening year of our forebears.

Julia Jones
Barbara Deer

MARCH

S layer of the winter, art thou here again?
O welcome, thou that bring'st the Summer nigh!
The bitter wind makes not the victory vain
Nor will we mock thee for thy faint blue sky.
Welcome, O March! Whose kindly days are dry.
Make April ready for the throstles' song,
Thou first redresser of the winters' wrong.

WILLIAM MORRIS

C ut daffodils should not be
mixed with other flowers as the
stems excrete a poisonous juice.

THE FLOWER GARDEN

Daffodil

THE DAFFODIL, along with the less romantic leek, is the national symbol of Wales. The pair are worn by loyal Welshmen on St. David's Day – the 1st of March. A charming Welsh tradition concerns the first bloom of the season – whoever is lucky enough to find it will, so legend has it, be blessed with more gold than silver. In other parts of Britain the first daffodil is thought to bring luck, but misfortune awaits those who would pluck a single bloom and bring it into the house.

On a more sombre note, the daffodil is credited with being the flower that carpeted the Elysian Fields – the legendary Field of the Dead – which may explain why the daffodil is so often seen decorating graves.

Strictly speaking, the daffodil is a trumpet narcissus. Modern methods of cultivation have ensured that we can enjoy these lovely blooms from Christmas to the end of May. They bring a welcome splash of colour when planted between shrubs and in the border.

Daffodowndilly has come to town
In a yellow petticoat and a green gown

THE FLOWER GARDEN

THE AURICULA or mountain cowslip was introduced to England in 1575. The old varieties have a lovely sweet scent and when picked will remain fresh for days. In Tudor times it was widely used as a cure for headaches.

THE POLYANTHUS is a cross between the cowslip and the primrose. The two species were combined to produce the quaintly-named oxslip, from which the polyanthus has been developed.

It is a mass of flowers, indeed its name comes from the Greek words for 'many flowered'. Popular in the 18th century, the 'gold-laced' varieties which were developed in the 1750s were the most highly prized and the polyanthus became the most widely grown of all cottage garden plants.

THE LENTEN ROSE, which flowers in March and April, is a close relation of the Christmas rose, and like the Christmas rose it is a poisonous plant. In medieval times its black roots were thought to have magical properties. It is a pretty plant and comes in a wide range of colours from green and white, through to purple and pink.

THE VIOLET has its place in politics as well as botany and herbal lore. It was the symbol of Athens as long ago as 1000 BC, and it was adopted as the emblem of the Imperial Napoleonic Party when Napoleon, known to his followers by the code name Caporal Violette, was exiled to Elba.

It is a flower that has long been associated with sleep. The herbalist Anthony Ascham declared 'for they that may not sleep, seep this herb in water and at eventide let him soak well his feet in the water to his ancles . . . and he shall sleep well by the grace of God.'

Violets do not grow well in towns or near factories as they need clear, clean air to flourish. For many centuries violets were sold in the streets of London and since medieval times violet blooms have been crystallized for cake decorations and as a sweetmeat.

That which above all yields the sweetest smell in the air is the violet.
SIR FRANCIS BACON

Violets are said to carry fleas in their stems, and in some parts of the country people will not bring the flowers into the house.

How to make
CRYSTALLIZED VIOLETS
large bunch of violets
1lb/500g caster sugar
1 cup of water
Remove violet heads from their stalks. Wash very carefully and pat dry with kitchen paper. Put the caster sugar and water into a saucepan over a medium heat and bring to the boil. Heat until the syrup reaches 240°F/120°C on a sugar thermometer. Continue to boil for one minute. Reduce the heat and drop in the flower heads, a few at a time. Leave to simmer for a further minute. Remove carefully with a slotted spoon. Drain well and place on a sheet of foil to cool. Turn at least once. Store in an airtight tin.

THE VEGETABLE GARDEN

RIDDING THE GARDEN OF SLUGS

One old method for getting rid of slugs is to take a good quantity of cabbage leaves, warm them in the stove or in front of a fire. When soft, spread them with dripping and lay them amongst your vegetables, they will soon be covered with slugs and snails which can then be disposed of.

Another method is to distribute saucers of beer around the vegetable plot. The slugs will climb in for a drink and find it impossible to leave.

In Ireland, young girls will search the garden for slugs. If the first one they find is a whitish colour, then their future bridegroom will be fair. If the slug is black, then the groom will be dark-haired.

TO DISCOURAGE MOLES

Stand unstoppered bottles about two or three yards (2 metres) apart in the moles' runs. The sound of the wind whistling in the bottlenecks will drive them away. A head of garlic or an onion stuck firmly down their runs will have the same effect.

PLANTING

March is the traditional time for planting hardy vegetables such as Brussels sprouts, parsnips, leeks and carrots. In Victorian times gardeners were advised to spit in the drill before planting their seeds.

Another piece of good advice was to plant potatoes and onions at opposite ends of the garden as 'the onions will make the taters cry their eyes out'.

For a good crop of potatoes it is suggested that they should be planted on a really stormy night.

An attractive and safe insect repellant for the home is a bunch of dried tansy flowers stripped of their leaves.

In March and in April, from morning to night,
In sowing and setting good housewives delight;
To have in a garden, or other like plot
To trim up their houses, and furnish their pot.

THOMAS TUSSER

THE RADISH was much prized by the ancient Greeks, who are reputed to have cast its image in gold for their temple at Delphi. The Egyptians are recorded as having eaten vast quantities of them, along with garlic and onions. Herbalists in Britain used the radish to cure kidney stones and to improve the workings of the bladder.

Young, crunchy radishes are at their best when served with nothing but a pat of best butter and a dish of sea salt.

SPINACH is a native of Persia. The Arabs are thought to have discovered it growing there and introduced it to Spain, from whence it found its way to Northern Europe.

Spinach is packed with vitamins and minerals and is, in fact, the most nourishing of all green vegetables, although it is high in oxalic acid and eating too much of it could cause problems. Careful planting will mean you can enjoy spinach all year round.

Radishes pulled up as the moon wanes will cure corns and warts.

VEGETABLE SEEDS.

Kidney Beans.

Phaseolus nanus.) German, Zwergbohne.—French, Haricot.

THE WILD HYACINTH, or bluebell, has a strange history. It is said that Apollo, god of the sun, had fallen in love with Hyacinthus, the handsome Prince of Sparta who was also loved by Zephyr, god of the winds. One day, Apollo and Hyacinthus were playing quoits, watched by the jealous Zephyr, who caused Apollo's quoit to swerve and hit Hyacinthus, killing the youth outright. The broken-hearted Apollo then formed the hyacinth flower out of the blood of his beloved. Even today, the Greeks say of the wild bluebell that grows there that the petals are marked with the Greek syllable, *ai, ai!* meaning woe, woe! However, our native woodland bluebell has no such mystic markings.

In times past it was said that a distillation from hyacinth bulbs could stop a boy's voice from breaking and this remedy was commonly administered by singing masters, although there is no scientific evidence to support this theory. The bulbs are, in fact, poisonous when fresh and they exude a sticky juice that was used by the Elizabethans as a starch for their ornate fluted ruffs.

When lifting and splitting clumps of snowdrops before replanting, it is important to reassure them that you are doing it for their own good, otherwise they will not thrive.

A shamrock will close its leaves at the approach of rain.

*The pious prune their roses on St. Patrick's Day,
The worldly on
Grand National Day.*

*Sweet peas sown on
St Patrick's Day
are said to produce larger
more fragrant blooms.*

*One leaf for fame,
One leaf for wealth,
One leaf for a faithful lover,
And one leaf to bring glorious health,
All are in a four-leafed clover.*

A MARCH CALENDAR

A windy March foretells a fine May.

March winds and April showers Bring forth May flowers.

1st March
ST. DAVID'S DAY

The national day of the Welsh. Legend has it that the Welsh victory over the Saxons in 640 AD was made possible by the fact that the Welsh wore leeks on their jackets and were thus able to recognise each other, whereas the Saxons without such a badge spent much of the battle fighting amongst themselves.

On this day fleas are said to return, so you would be well advised to keep doors and windows closed on St. David's Day.

2nd March
ST. CHAD'S DAY

Sow peas and beans on David and Chad. Be the weather good or bad.

COUNTRY RHYME

17th March

ST. PATRICK'S DAY

Patrick, the patron saint of Ireland spent the greater part of his life establishing churches all over Ireland. He died there in 461 AD. St. Patrick is supposed to have disliked snakes and banished them from Ireland – there are, in fact, no native Irish snakes. Patrick also put a curse on ferns – maybe because it was thought that the wearing of a sprig of fern would cause you to be followed by all manner of reptiles. His symbol was the trefoil (shamrock or clover) which he used to demonstrate the idea of the Holy Trinity. A gardening chore to be tackled today is the pruning of roses.

How to make
FLORAL EASTER EGGS

6 white eggs
assorted food colourings
¼ pint/150ml malt vinegar
a little extra egg white
small flat flowers and leaves
scrap of fine cotton or muslin
fine thread or string
(This method will not
work on brown eggs.)

Place the eggs in a saucepan of cold water and bring gently to the boil. Allow to simmer for about twenty minutes. Remove and plunge into a bowl of cold water for about five minutes. Remove and dry thoroughly.

Mix together 20 drops of food colouring, two teaspoons of vinegar and 10 floz/300ml of boiling water. Make up as many colours as desired. Steep the eggs in the prepared solutions until the eggs are a pale but solid colour. Remove with a slotted spoon and place in an egg carton to dry.

Using the extra egg white, stick small flat flower heads and leaves to the egg. Wrap carefully, but tightly with fine muslin and secure with thread.

Dip each egg into a solution of a different colour. Again leave until the required colour is obtained. Remove with a slotted spoon and leave to dry in the egg carton.

When completely dry, remove the cotton or muslin, the flowers and the leaves and polish each egg with a little cooking oil or butter. Pile into a pretty dish and use as a table decoration.

MOTHERING SUNDAY

Originally, Mothering Sunday was instituted by the church as the day on which people went to visit their 'mother' church, the cathedral of their diocese, on the 4th Sunday in Lent. In the 17th century the day became associated with the honouring of mothers. The traditional gift for Mothering Sunday is a bunch of flowers. Country girls in service would be allowed home on this day and would often pick a bunch of spring flowers as they walked home. Primroses and violets would have been popular choices.

6th Sunday in Lent
PALM SUNDAY

On this day keen gardeners were advised to sweep out the church, scattering the dust onto the garden to protect and fertilize the soil. This was considered a good day for planting seeds.

Friday before Easter
GOOD FRIDAY

This is the day of Christ's crucifixion, the most solemn day of the Christian year. No flowers or plants are used to decorate the church, but a sprig of yew may be hung up to signify mourning.

In the gardens of the south no potatoes should be planted on Good Friday and bee hives should never be moved on this inauspicious day. However, in the Midlands this day was known as 'Spud Day' – the day for planting potatoes.

EASTER SUNDAY

Easter is a moveable feast – it can fall anywhere between 21st March and the 25th April. The date is fixed by the first full moon on or after 21st March.

A plant with special significance for Easter Sunday is the sweet bay, which has been chosen to represent the resurrection because of its ability to grow again from the roots after seeming to have died.

BORROWING DAYS

The last three days in March are called 'blind days' and no seeds should be planted. The weather is often windy and stormy at this time and tradition has it that these days have been 'borrowed' from April.

March borrowed from April
Three days, and they were ill
The first was snow and sleet
The next was cold and weet
The third was sic a freeze
The birds' nests stuck to trees.

APRIL

April, the angel of the months, the young
Love of the Year. Ancient and still so young
Lovelier than the craven's paradox;
Christ's Easter and the Syrian Adonis,
When all things turn into their contrary,
Death into life and silence into sound.

VITA SACKVILLE-WEST

Buttercups and daisies,
Oh, the pretty flowers;
Coming ere the Spring-time,
To tell of sunny hours.

MARY HOWITT

THE FLOWER GARDEN

Daisy

AN EMBLEM of fidelity and innocence, daisies were thought by the Celts to be the spirits of children who died at birth. In some parts of the country it is considered very unlucky to step on a daisy and even more dangerous to uproot a plant, as it foretold that your children would not prosper. It was widely believed that a nursing child would become stunted if it should touch a daisy and if daisies were fed to unweaned puppies they would not thrive.

Its leaves contain an acrid juice which was used in Elizabethan times as a remedy for gout and rheumatism and, sniffed up the nose, as a cure for migraine. On account of its bitter flavour, insects and cattle avoid the daisy completely.

In Scotland, it is called the bairnwort because of the pleasure that the making of daisy chains has given to generation after generation of children.

Spring has come when you can put your foot on three daisies.

19

LEOPARD'S BANE, also known as arnica, is a native of Central Europe and was introduced to Britain by the invading Roman armies. It owes its strange name to the medieval practice of mixing its dried root, which is extremely poisonous, with bait, in order to rid the countryside of unwanted vermin. It does have a less lethal use – a few drops of tincture of leopard's bane added to a basin of hot water makes an excellent foot bath.

Leopard's bane makes a striking border plant for the cottage garden. A particularly lovely variety is 'Spring Beauty' which produces double blooms of a vibrant buttery yellow.

AUBRETIA takes its name from the French botanist, Aubriet, who found it growing to striking effect among rock formations in Greece. It was introduced to Britain in 1710 and soon became a cottage garden favourite. It is an ideal rockery plant that blooms early and attracts brimstone butterflies.

Soak flower seeds in scented water and dry them in the sun. When the plants grow they will retain their borrowed perfume.

Solomon's seal is said to be the 'husband' of lily of the valley – plant the two together and your garden will be filled with harmony.

The first spring-blown anemone,
She in his doublet wove,
To keep him safe from pestilence
Wherever he should rove.

OLD ENGLISH BALLAD

Cut tulips will last longer if the
flowers are wrapped in newspaper
and allowed to stand up to their
neck in water for a few hours.

If you'd enjoy the fruit,
pluck not the flower

SOLOMON'S SEAL is thought by many to be the most lovely of the old-fashioned cottage garden plants, yet it is rarely seen today. Its unusual name derives from the markings on its stem, which when cut through are said to resemble the seal of King Solomon.

The plant was very popular with Tudor herbalists who used it to cure bruises received 'by woman's wilfulness in stumbling upon their nasty husband's fists'. The ladies of the Italian courts used a toilet water distilled from the pretty greenish-white flowers to keep their complexions clear and ever youthful.

THE ANEMONE is a beautiful, but scentless, spring flower. The first flower of the season was prized by the early herbalists for its healing properties. The flower was wrapped in a scarlet cloth and tied to the arm of a sick person with the chant: 'I gathered thee for a remedy against disease'.

TULIPS were introduced to Western Europe from Turkey in the middle of the 16th century. The Dutch developed a passion for them, rival bulb-growers vied with each other to produce more and more exotic varieties and colours and bulbs changed hands for enormous prices.

Tulips will not thrive if left in the same spot for more than two years running. They should be allowed to die back, and then be moved to fresh soil otherwise they can become affected with a disease known as 'tulip fire'.

FROGS AND TOADS

A still pond makes an ideal breeding ground for frogs, toads and newts. If you wish to encourage them, you could provide a gentle slope or ramp, or a patch of overhanging vegetation to make it easier for the young frog to emerge from the water. A few stones or rocks will provide a welcome place of hibernation for the winter months.

Be prepared for a lot of noise, male frogs and toads gather together in raucous groups making as much noise as they can to attract the females. They will return to their breeding grounds every year, even if the pond they call home has been filled in.

Frogs will repay your hospitality by gobbling up slugs, snails and other garden pests as they roam about the garden at night.

CUCKOO! CUCKOO!

In Scotland, the number of calls you heard the cuckoo make was believed to foretell the number of years you had left to live. In parts of the Midlands it was said that if a maiden ran into the fields early on an April morning to hear the cuckoo's call, she should take off her left shoe and in it she would find a man's hair, of the same colour as that of her future husband.

If you hear a cuckoo for the first time on April 28th, you will enjoy a year of prosperity, but if you are a-bed when you hear the first cuckoo, then someone in your family will die before the year is out. Turning over the coins in your pockets at the sound will ensure that you will never be poor.

WEEDS

It may be a comfort to know that in the 18th century, weeds were thought a 'useless abundance' and it was believed that they grew at God's command as a punishment for the sins of Adam. It was considered impious to attempt to rid the garden of them completely, as this was seen as an act of rebellion against the Creator.

Butterflies

These attractive garden visitors wake up in the spring to lay their eggs and are ravenous for nectar. They can be encouraged into the garden by providing them with nectar-rich flowers and some suitable food for their caterpillars.

Buddleia, also known as the butterfly bush, is particularly attractive to butterflies, especially to red admirals, tortoiseshells and whites. They also like wallflowers, sweet rocket, catmint, lavender and ice plants.

Caterpillars are, of course, less welcome as they can be destructive, they enjoy amongst other things, clover, privet, gorse, cabbages, bramble, blackthorn, beech and willow leaves.

The caterpillar on the leaf
Repeats to thee thy mother's grief.
Kill not the moth nor butterfly,
For the Last Judgement draweth nigh.

WILLIAM BLAKE

An APRIL CALENDAR

1st April
ALL FOOL'S DAY

This day is thought to commemorate the fruitless mission of the rook, who was sent out in search of land from Noah's flood-encircled ark. In fact, the time-honoured method of making an 'April fool' is to send the person on a fool's errand – to gather hen's teeth, or striped paint or pigeon's milk or some such non-existent thing.

A bird associated with April Fool's Day is the cuckoo, which is usually heard for the first time this month.

First Sunday in April
DAFFODIL SUNDAY

The Victorians liked to make excuses for going out walking and they invented special days for doing just that. The first Sunday in April was a day when families would walk out together to pick daffodils from their gardens and take them to local hospitals to give to the sick.

When clouds appear like rocks and towers
The earth's refreshed by frequent showers.

KENT WEATHER RHYME

19th April
PRIMROSE DAY

The primrose was the favourite flower of Prime Minister Disraeli and on his birthday Queen Victoria sent him vast quantities of them. Disraeli is said to have thanked Her Majesty, perhaps a trifle sarcastically, for giving him gold instead of the honours and awards she bestowed upon others. So much did Disraeli love the primrose that after his death on April 19th, 1881, Primrose Day was inaugurated, and in 1883 Lady Randolph Churchill founded The Primrose League to further the cause of Conservatism.

23rd April
ST. GEORGE'S DAY

On this day young men would go to the woods and bring back green boughs to dress up one of their number as Jack-in-the-Green, the spirit of Spring. He would feature in their Morris dances and May Day celebrations.

The flower associated with St. George's Day is, of course, the rose – the flower of England.

25th April
ST. MARK'S DAY

The Evangelist Saint Mark is, supposedly, the patron saint of mildew. Now is the time to pray if your garden is blighted by this disease and all other remedies have failed.

When April rain had laughed the land
Out of its wintery way,
And coaxed all growing things to greet
With gracious garb the May.

SHAEMUS O'SHEEL

If, when you first hear the cuckoo, you mark well where your right foot standeth, and take up of that earth, the fleas will by no means breed where any of that same earth is scattered

THOMAS HYLL

THE VEGETABLE GARDEN
PLANTING LORE

The Greeks and Romans believed that sap in plants waxed and waned with the moon, and in fact scientists have now proved that all water moves in a lunar rhythm, like the sea. So old wives' tale or no, it makes sense to plant with a waxing moon.

An ancient country practice involved the gardener removing his trousers and sitting on the ground before sowing in order to ascertain the temperature of the soil. If it was too cold for naked flesh, it would be too cold for the seeds. Many ancient gardening manuals suggest sowing seed when naked, but this is probably a relic of ancient fertility customs.

It was considered unlucky for a woman to plant large numbers of lettuces in her garden. If she was single, it would mean that she would never marry and if married, but childless, it would mean that she would never conceive.

In Cheshire, many gardeners awaited the arrival of the yellow wagtail, which arrives here from the continent in April, before they would risk planting their potatoes. For this reason the yellow wagtail was known as the potato dropper, presumably from the action of its tail. Elsewhere the size of the elm tree leaf was used as a signal for planting kidney beans.

In the decay of the moon,
A cloudy morn bodes a fair afternoon.

DEVON AND DORSET RHYME

KALE is a cabbage green and a somewhat neglected vegetable these days. The Romans and Greeks, whose climate was too warm to grow cabbages successfully, enjoyed it and the Victorian gardener considered it an essential standby in the vegetable garden, suitable for both kitchen use and for livestock.

Curly kale is the better tasting variety, it has crimped leaves and it should be washed thoroughly under running water before cooking.

Some varieties of kale are grown as ornamental plants, and there is one particular type that has stems so hard and woody that in country districts they are dried and used as walking sticks.

Plant kidney beans, if you be so willing,
When elm leaves are as big as a shilling,
When elm leaves are as big as a penny,
You must plant beans if you mean to have any.

BROCCOLI is often thought of as a cauliflower with many heads, and in fact that is its advantage over cauliflower – its heads can be picked a few at a time, thus allowing for a longer period of enjoyment. It takes up quite a lot of space in the kitchen garden so it makes sense to grow only winter and spring varieties.

When you hear the cuckoo shout
'Tis time to plant your tatties out

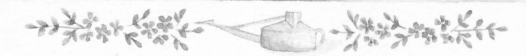

MAY

To rise from sloth, as ye from winter's night,
Rejoicing garden-land and forest dell;
With all the soul, with all the heart and might,
Aiding brotherhood in which we dwell.
To learn of sweetest May, and kindly give
Blessings with open hand to all that live!

ANON

A lily of a day
Is fairer far in May,
Although it fall and die that night;
It was the plant and flower of light.
In small proportions we just beauties see;
And in short measures, life may perfect be.

BEN JONSON

THE FLOWER GARDEN

Lily of the Valley

IN IRELAND the delicate bells of the lily of the valley have earned it the name fairy ladders as it was thought that the 'little people' climbed them. It is also known as ladder to heaven and Jacob's ladder and is often used as a symbol of Christ's second coming. Its sweet scent was thought to lure the nightingale into the woods to choose its mate.

Other legends associated with this beautiful flower are that they sprang from the tears that Mary shed at the foot of the cross and that the distinctive scent has the power to help men see a better world.

In the 16th century John Gerard, the herbalist, wrote of a precious elixir obtained from putting lily of the valley into a glass and the covered glass into an anthill for one month. The liquid which resulted was credited with being a sovereign remedy for gout. The elixir was believed to be more valuable than gold and was called *eau d'or* for that reason. Its value may have been enhanced because of the belief that a little smear of the elixir on the forehead and back of the neck would impart that most valuable of human qualities – common sense.

See bending to the gentle gale,
The modest lily of the vale;
Hid in its leaf of tender green,
Mark its soft and simple mien.

MRS HEMANS

BLEEDING HEART is named after the fanciful suggestion that the blossom resembles a heart shedding a single drop of blood. It is a native of America that was introduced into England in 1846 by the botanist Robert Fortune. It has since become established as a popular English border plant, and it is a lovely sight with its arching branchlets carrying delicate magenta and white flowers.

As a medicinal herb, it has been found to have slight narcotic properties and was used in the past as a remedy for venereal diseases and menstrual cramps.

GYPSOPHILA, or baby's breath, are lovely dainty flowers that look wonderful dried. Cut the blooms on a dry day when they are at their best. Tie them into bunches and hang upside down in a dark airy place until they are completely dry and papery.

THE FOXGLOVE is perfectly designed for pollination by the honey-bee. The projecting lower part of the flower bell provides a landing platform for the bee and as he works his way up into the bell towards the nectar, pollen is rubbed on his back by the stamens above him.

The foxglove contains digitalis, a powerful and important drug used in the treatment of heart disease and circulatory disorders. Foxgloves are cultivated for digitalis in parts of England and Germany.

According to northern legend, wicked fairies gave these flowers to foxes so that they could slip their paws into them and prowl quietly around the chicken runs. The marks on the blossoms are said to be the finger prints of the mischievous elves.

Then came fair May,
The Fayrest mayd on ground
Dekt all with dainties of her season's pryde:
And throwing flowers out of her lap around:
Upon two brethren's shoulders she did ride,
The twinnes Leda; which on either side
Supported her like to their Soveraine Queene.

EDMUND SPENSER

The markings on the blossoms of the foxglove are a warning sign of the poisonous juices within.

YARROW belongs to the genus *Achillea*, which was named after Achilles, hero of Homer's Illiad. It is said that he used yarrow to bind the wounds of his soldiers and that it helped to staunch the flow of blood. Modern research has found that the yarrow does indeed contain blood-clotting chemicals, and this would account for its old names of bloodwort, soldier's woundwort and staunchweed.

Yarrow is a good garden tonic, one or two plants planted around the garden should increase the aroma and flavour of their neighbours.

There is a particularly pretty variety, ideal for the English cottage garden, which is called 'Sweet Nancy' – it has large white flowers and pretty silvery-grey foliage.

Good morrow, good morrow,
Sweet yarrow to you.
If I see my true love in white
His love to me is ever bright.
If he appears to me in blue,
His love to me is ever true.
If he appears to me in black,
His love to me will lack.

MAY EVE RHYME

Under the spreading chestnut tree
The village smithy stands;
The smith a mighty man is he,
With large and sinewy hands.

HENRY W. LONGFELLOW

How to make
YARROW INFUSION

The following is said to be a cure for baldness:
A handful fresh yarrow leaves and flowers
10fl oz/300ml boiling water
Wash the yarrow leaves and flowers in cold water. Drain well and put into a large jug. Pour over the boiling water and cover with a folded towel. Leave to infuse for 10 to 15 minutes. Strain and bottle. Rub into the scalp four or five times a week!

Black knight-at-arms,
The white-plumed Thorn;
In pomp the Crown Imperial born.

WALTER CRANE

CROWN IMPERIAL is so called because of the majesty of its blooms which are carried on stems up to three feet tall. It has other royal connections – it is said to have bloomed for the first time in Europe in the garden of an Austrian Emperor.

The flower is a native of Persia (now Iran) and according to the folklore of that country, the drop of nectar contained in each blossom is not nectar but the tears of a beautiful queen, unjustly accused of being unfaithful to her husband. To protect her from his wrath, an angel turned the queen into a flower which will continue to cry until she and her husband are happily re-united.

A Christian legend has it that this flower refused to bow its head on Good Friday as Christ passed by and was condemned to cry forever – its tears not falling even in the strongest of winds.

The bulb has a rather unpleasant odour, it has been likened to the stench of a fox's den and it is known in some areas, somewhat unkindly, as the stink lily.

Despite the sad legends and the less than flattering names, crown imperial makes an attractive spring-flowering border plant that can be left in the same position, year after year.

And do you ask me why this flower
Is fit for every brow?
Tell me but one where Folly n'er
Hath dwellt, nor dwelleth now.

ANON. FOLLY'S FLOWER – THE COLUMBINE

THE CORNFLOWER is a favourite among cottage garden flowers. It was popular in Tudor gardens where it was grown in a variety of colours other than the beautiful blue we associate it with today.

Farmers have never been fond of the cornflower. It was believed to spring up from wheat seeds causing a poor harvest. In fact they do leach the soil of nutrients needed for corn, but it is their tough stems that are the farmer's true enemy. An ancient name for the plant is 'hurt-sickle' because a patch of cornflowers could blunt the sharpest sickle.

COLUMBINE takes its name from the Latin word *columba*, a dove, the flower being thought to resemble a dove's head. In ancient times it was widely believed that lions would eat columbine flowers in spring for their strength-giving properties and because of this the herbalist Gerard referred to Columbine as *Herba Leonis*.

In the 17th century it was considered very indiscreet to give Columbine to a woman as it was associated with a certain looseness of morals. The flower also fares badly by association in the Language of Flowers – columbine is a symbol of foolishness, the shape of the flower being likened to a jester's cap.

The juice squeezed from the
petals of the cornflower and mixed
with alum-water makes a
beautiful water-colour paint.

TREES AND SHRUBS

THE HAWTHORN gets its name from the Old English meaning hedge thorn and it does indeed make a very strong, fine hedge. It is also known as may, and in medieval times, the cutting of may blossom had great symbolism. It signified the bringing of new life and the onset of the growing season. Garlands of may blossoms were carried from door to door to share out the benefits of this great creative surge of power.

The popular rhyme 'Here we go gathering nuts in May' is thought to have its origins in the song sung by the young men gathering not 'nuts' in May (which is most unlikely) but 'knots' of may for the May Day celebrations. Hawthorn was used to decorate front doors on May Day, but it was considered a sure sign of death to take the blossoms into the house.

In Northamptonshire, a hawthorn branch was stuck into the ground in the garden of the prettiest girl of the village – obviously a charming relic of some ancient fertility rite.

THE LABURNUM is often seen in country gardens. It is an ornamental tree about twenty feet high that in May is covered by long chains of flowers, hence its popular names golden chain, golden rain and watch and chain.

The wood of the laburnum tree is dark and takes a high polish. It is used for good quality furniture and for musical instruments. The seeds of the laburnum tree contain a deadly poison that has featured in many a murder mystery – children should be warned never to touch them.

How to make
MAY BLOSSOM WINE

the grated rind of two lemons (well scrubbed)
juice of one lemon
4.5 litres/1 gallon water
sauterne yeast – follow maker's instructions per gallon/litre
Nutrient – 3 × 3mg tablets of Vitamin B1 per gallon
2 quarts/2.25 kilos of washed hawthorn flowers

Put the lemon rind, juice and water into a saucepan and boil for 30 minutes. Pour into a wine-maker's bucket. Leave to cool to 70°F/21°C and add yeast and nutrient. Cover and leave for 24 hours. Add hawthorn flowers. Stir, cover and leave to stand for eight days, stirring well every day. On the ninth day strain through a sieve into a fermenting jar and fit an air-lock. Leave to ferment until the wine clears. Rack and replace in the fermenting jar. Leave for a further three months. Rack and bottle in the normal way.

THE LILAC is said to have first bloomed in Scotland – the seed having been dropped into an old lady's garden by a falcon. This seed grew into a beautiful bush but it did not flower. One day a prince stopped to admire the bush and a plume from his hat fell into it. From that day, the lilac bore purple flowers.

But the story does not end there. A young girl in the neighbourhood died on the eve of her marriage. She so loved the lilac in the old lady's garden that she asked for a cutting to be planted on her grave. The bush that bloomed bore white flowers.

Superstitions about white lilac persist to this day. In some parts of the country it is considered unlucky to wear white lilac, except on May Day, as it means one will never marry.

THE WISTERIA was brought to this country from China and Japan. The beautiful fragrant flowers are very similar to those of the laburnum, indeed they are from the same family, and the roots and bark of the Chinese wisteria are poisonous. Wisteria is a vigorous climber which will need to be supported if grown on a wall but it will self-climb over a pergola.

Knots of may we've brought you,
Before your door it stands;
It is but a sprout,
But it's well budded out
By the work of the Lord's hand.

LONDON MAY GIRLS' SONG

And in the warm hedge grew lush eglantine,
Green cow-bind and the moonlight-
coloured may.

PERCY BYSSHE SHELLEY

A MAY CALENDAR

1st May
MAY DAY

The month of May is named after the Greek goddess Maia, the eldest of the Pleiades and mother of Hermes. The celebrations that we know as May Day have their origins in the rites of Spring and the ceremonies and sacrifices due to the equivalent Roman goddess, Maia Majesta, on the first day of her month.

In more recent times, the May Day dances have featured a Queen of the May, a modern representation of Maia. In some areas the girl is called Maid Marion, a confusion that seems to date from the 15th and 16th centuries, but call her what you will, the symbolism of a young, fertile girl at the centre of the celebrations is inescapable. The maypole around which the girls dance is a relic of our tree-worshipping past. These ceremonies, therefore neatly join together the old religions of the Romans and the Druids.

Sunday before Ascension Day
CHESTNUT SUNDAY

This is another Victorian invention – an excuse for middle-class families to travel to Kew and Bushey to view the spectacle of the horse-chestnuts in bloom.

The horse-chestnut is one of the first trees to open in spring. It flowers in late May and early June, making the tree look like a giant candelabra – in fact the horse chestnut is sometimes known as the candle-tree.

40 days after Easter
ASCENSION DAY

In many areas it was believed that no work should be done in the garden on this day, for to do so would result in poor and blighted crops. Some, however, consider this the best day to plant sweet peas as long as the work is done before dawn.

In parts of Wales it was considered fatal to do work of any sort on this day.

Bring orchis, bring the foxglove spire,
The little speedwell's darling blue,
Deep tulips dash'd with fiery dew,
Laburnums, dropping wells of fire.

ALFRED, LORD TENNYSON

19th May
ST DUNSTAN'S DAY

A frost in mid-May can prove disastrous for fruit blossom, and in some years late frosts do occur around this date. This has given rise to the legend that St. Dunstan made a pact with the devil which ensures that apple and pear blossoms will be spared nine years out of ten, and in the tenth year the frost will come on St. Dunstan's day.

29th May
OAK APPLE DAY

On this day in 1660 Charles II reclaimed his throne. Until the beginning of this century, it was common practice to wear a sprig of oak leaves and an oak apple to demonstrate one's allegiance to the crown. During his exile in France his supporters had adopted the oak as a symbol of the monarchy after Charles' famous hiding place in the oak tree at Boscobel, in Shropshire.

St. Dunstan, as the story goes,
Once pulled the devil by his nose
With red hot tongs, which made him roar,
That could be heard ten miles or more.

CHILDREN'S RHYME

If your fruit trees are affected with leaf curl,
pick off affected leaves and hang a few mothballs
among the branches.

A Laburnum tree should never overhang pasture land, it could prove fatal to grazing sheep and cattle.

First April, she with mellow showers,
Opens the way for early flowers:
Then after her comes smiling May
In a more rich and sweet array.

ROBERT HERRICK

THE HERB GARDEN

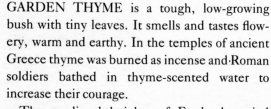

SWEET MARJORAM has a lovely aroma that is very attractive to bees. To the Greeks it was known as 'joy of the mountains'; while the Romans offered bunches of this herb as a symbol of peace and friendship.

A tisane of marjoram can be used to soothe sore throats and colds and, in the kitchen, a blend of thyme and marjoram is particularly good with tomatoes.

GARDEN THYME is a tough, low-growing bush with tiny leaves. It smells and tastes flowery, warm and earthy. In the temples of ancient Greece thyme was burned as incense and·Roman soldiers bathed in thyme-scented water to increase their courage.

The medieval knights of England carried favours embroidered with sprigs of thyme. Whilst in the reign of Queen Anne, thyme and beer soup was a recognised cure for shyness!

How to make
A FAGGOT OF HERBS
Take a bay leaf, two sprigs of parsley and a sprig each of thyme and marjoram. Make the herbs into a little bunch and tie securely together with fine cotton or string.
Use in chicken and meat dishes.

How to make
A BUNDLE OF SWEET HERBS
Take two sprigs each of sweet cicely and lemon balm and one sprig of lemon thyme. Tie into a bundle with a small piece of fresh angelica stem. Use in syrup for fruit salad and in fruit cups and puddings.

Thyme is a good companion plant to the cabbage.

Who doffs his coat on a Winter's day Will gladly put it on in May.

THE VEGETABLE GARDEN

May is the month for planting out Brussels sprouts, a stick of rhubarb planted alongside each plant will prevent club-root. Onions can still be sown in May – they will benefit from a top dressing of soot. Dig trenches now for early crops of celery and plant out on a showery day for best results.

ASPARAGUS is a close relation of the lily of the valley and has been cultivated since Egyptian times. In this country it is associated with the lavish kitchen gardens of great houses, but, in fact, it is quite an easy crop to grow provided the gardener has patience, as an asparagus bed takes several years to establish itself.

Plant three-year-old roots and do not cut them until the second year. When ready to harvest, cut with a saw-bladed knife and harvest all your asparagus before Midsummer's Day, what is left thereafter will be hard and woody.

There is no flavour to compare with asparagus fresh from the garden, cut and cooked within the hour – asparagus starts to lose its flavour the minute it is cut.

Be it weal or be it woe
Beans blow before May go.

Ambassadors cropped up like hay,
Prime Ministers and such as they
Grew like asparagus in May,
And dukes were three a penny.

W. S. GILBERT

JUNE

Come honey-bee, with thy busy hum,
To the fragrant tufts of wild thyme come,
And sip the sweet dew from the cowslip's head,
From the lily's bell and the violet's bed.

ANON

What's in a name? That
which we call a rose, by any
other name would smell as
sweet.

W. SHAKESPEARE

A clove of garlic, planted
near a rose bush will ward off
greenfly and will not affect the
rose's wonderful perfume.

A cure for aphids: Steep
half a pound of best tobacco
in a gallon of hot water.
When the infusion is cold,
paint the affected rose leaves
and then rinse with clear
water.

THE FLOWER GARDEN
Rose

THE ROSE has been cultivated since biblical times. It was a symbol of all things pleasurable to the Romans and Greeks who liberally scattered the flowers beneath the chariot wheels of homecoming victors, in the wine goblets of the rich and exalted and atop the heads of lovers. In English history the hedonistic image of this beautiful perfumed flower was somewhat bloodied by the War of Roses which raged between the white rose of York, and the red rose of Lancaster.

Henry Tudor, the victor in that war, took as his emblem a rose that united the two roses and this Tudor rose has been the symbol of the British monarchy ever since.

Many classic old roses have been cultivated in this country for centuries and are still available today. *Eglantine* or the *Sweet Briar* rose is one of our few native roses, producing beautiful pale pink flowers with a delicate perfume. You can still grow a rose very similar to the original *White Rose of York*, it is a bushy variety that requires little pruning. The red rose of Lancaster goes under the name of *Apothecary's Rose*, it was much prized for its medicinal properties and its strong perfume. *The Damask Rose* is perhaps the most ancient of all. It is to be found depicted on the walls of the Palace of Knossos, Crete, which dates back to 2000 BC. This rose is grown for its essential oil known as Attar of Roses and used extensively in perfumery.

GERANIUMS of the cultivated kind are synonymous with colour and sunshine. The wild form of geranium, called Herb Robert, is deep pink and can be found in hedgerows. Its name may refer to the legendary woodsprite, Robin Goodfellow, the forerunner of Robin Hood, who played tricks on evil-doers and helped honest people

There once was a doormouse who lived in a bed
Of delphiniums (blue) and geraniums (red),
And all the day long he'd a wonderful view
Of generaniums (red) and delphiniums (blue).

A. A. MILNE

Here are sweet peas,
on tiptoe for a flight
With wings of gentle flush
o'er delicate white.

JOHN KEATS

THE BEGONIA, a species of brightly-coloured flowering plant, was named after the French Governor of the West Indies and amateur botanist, Michel Begon. Begonias like sunshine and moisture and they need to be protected from the rigours of an English winter by being potted up and transferred to the greenhouse in the colder months. In the Victorian Language of Flowers the begonia means dark thoughts, a strange interpretation for such a bright plant.

THE SWEET PEA is a climbing plant, and an essential element in every cottage garden, it was greatly loved by the Victorians. It became so popular that in 1901 the English National Sweet Pea Society was formed and this flower became the symbol of Edwardian England.

THE PEONY, well known for its medicinal properties, is named after the Greek physician Paeon. The seeds have been used as a cooking spice, as a remedy for the pains of childbirth, as a necklace to ward off evil spirits and, steeped in wine, as a cure for nightmares. Dried and ground peony root is a recognised anti-spasmodic and has been successfully used in the treatment of epilepsy and other nervous afflictions.

The peony plant will last a lifetime if left undisturbed after planting. Legend has it that uprooting the plant will bring extremes of bad luck, and the only way to retrieve the prized root is to get a dog to dig it up in the dead of night.

Do not cut support canes from an ash tree, as the tendrils of the sweet pea recoil from the touch of the magical ash.

A JUNE CALENDAR

8th June
If on the eighth of June it rain
That foretells a wet harvest, men sayen.

11th June
ST BARNABAS'S DAY

This was the longest day before the calendar change of 1752. On this day it was customary to deck churches and houses with roses and sweet woodruff 'being made up into garlands or bundles and hanged up in houses in the heat of Summer, doth very well attemper the air, cool and make fresh the place to the delight and comfort of such as are therein'. John Gerard 1633

15th June
ST VITUS'S DAY

If St. Vitus day be rainy weather
It will rain for forty days together.

23rd June
MIDSUMMER'S EVE

This is the night when witches and fairies are supposed to be particularly active, so it is a fitting time to take a few precautions against the one and enlist the help of the other.

To protect your home against evil spirits, make a garland of the 'herbs of St. John' – St. John's wort, plantain, corn marigold, yarrow and ivy – and burn it on the Midsummer fire. Hazel twigs cut on Midsummer's Eve are supposed to be particularly good for water divining.

Flees contracted on St. David's Day can be removed by jumping over the Midsummer bonfire.

24th June
MIDSUMMER'S DAY
THE FEAST OF ST JOHN

An old fortune-telling game for Midsummer's Day involves picking a handful of grass with the eyes closed. The number of daisies in the bunch indicates the years before marriage or, for a married person, the number of children they will have.

How to make
PRESERVED FLOWERS

Spread a layer of borax evenly over a baking tray and leave in a warm place until completely dry.
Tip dried borax into a shoe box to a depth of 1in/2.5cm. Place the flowers on top and sieve over more borax, very gently, until each flower is completely covered. Cup-shaped flowers should be filled with borax before being covered. Leave the box in a warm, dry place for up to five days.
To check whether a flower is dry enough, hold it carefully to the ear and flick gently. It should sound like paper. Leave the dried flowers in a dry room for a couple of hours and then remove excess borax very carefully with a paintbrush. Kept out of direct sunlight, the dried flowers should last well.

SWEET WOODRUFF is a pretty woodland plant particularly associated with midsummer festivities. Its lovely new-mown-hay scent develops as it dries. It was much used in pot-pourri and as a stuffing for pillows and mattresses.

THE VEGETABLE GARDEN

The vegetable garden should now be producing its first crops of peas and beans.

PEAS are particularly well-suited to the climate of Britain where they have long been a favourite vegetable. Until Tudor times, peas were eaten dried and then boiled in the form of pease pudding. In large kitchen gardens, the first crop of peas was expected by June 4th, King George III's birthday.

There are several superstitions attached to the shelling of peas. While it is considered good luck to find a pod containing a single pea, the luckiest pod of all is one containing nine perfect peas. If an unmarried girl puts such a pod on the lintel of the outer door, the first man to cross the threshold will be her future husband.

A swarm of bees in June is worth a silver spoon.

Plant strawberries near borage, beans and lettuces for their mutual benefit.

Peas and beans do well in the company of carrots, leeks and turnips, neither of them thrive in the proximity of onions, garlic or gladioli.

To protect seedlings from byrdes, antes, field mice and other spoylers of the garden, sprinkle with juice of houseleek on seed before sowing.

THOMAS HYLL

VEGETABLE SEEDS

Vegetable Marrow.
(*Cucurbita ovifera*.) German, *Kleiner Kürbiß.*
—French, *Courge à la Moëlle.*

The month of June is remarkable for the brilliancy of its sunlight, steady barometer, and even temperature.
For those who are engaged in gardening it provides plenty to occupy their time, as much work requires attention in all departments.

THE GARDEN ORACLE, 1896.

Mice will not destroy the seeds of peas and beans that have been rolled in paraffin.

Put hair clippings or horsehair teased from old mattresses into the bottom of bean trenches before sowing, and your beans will thrive.

Sow beans in the mud, they'll grow like wood.

BROAD BEANS are the traditional beans of England, and the ones referred to in the saying 'having a bean feast'. For a long time they were the staple diet of the poor and so were shunned by the more affluent.

Beans are associated with the dead whose souls are believed to live within the flowers. This connection has given rise to the superstition among colliers in the North and Midlands that coal-mining accidents are more likely when beans are in flower. The strong scent of the flowers is thought to induce madness, bad dreams and terrible visions.

THE FRUIT GARDEN

*Doubtless God
could have made a better berry,
but doubtless God never did.*

DR. WILLIAM BUTLER

THE STRAWBERRY, the fat and juicy garden variety, reached England from the New World in the 16th century. The tiny wild woodland berries native to Britain have been tangled in the undergrowth of hedges and country gardens for centuries. These wild strawberries grow almost like a weed and, for the expenditure of some labour in the picking, yield a fruit of superior flavour and fragrance.

An infusion made from strawberry leaves is recommended for the rheumatic. The juice of the fruit, if left on the teeth for about five minutes and then rinsed off with water containing a pinch of bicarbonate of soda, will remove discolouration. The same bleaching properties can be applied to the skin – a cut strawberry rubbed over the face immediately after washing will whiten the skin and lessen the marks of sunburn.

*To dream of strawberries is a
good omen. For a man it foretells
a docile wife and many children.*

CURRANT BUSHES flower early and attract the honey bee into the garden – a hard-working nectar-gatherer who will pollinate all kinds of plants as it goes about its business. The source of attraction may be the strongly-smelling leaves and buds. Goats are particularly partial to black currant leaves. Red currants make a wonderfully fragrant wine and a delicious jelly, in fact all the currants make excellent jams and jellies.

*Plant currant bushes in an old
nettle bed, or let nettles grow
between the bushes, this will
strengthen them against
disease.*

THE HERB GARDEN

Pick herbs now for drying and freezing. Gather them on a sunny day, after the dew has evaporated, but before the sun becomes too strong. Hang up the bunches in a dry, airy place or pack into plastic bags or containers and freeze.

SUMMER SAVORY is a sweet, aromatic herb used to flavour white meat, fish and vegetables. It is particularly good with broad beans as it is said to enhance their flavour and aid digestion. In times past summer savory was used not only as a culinary herb but also as a remedy for stomach disorders and fevers. Use the tops of the early spring seedlings now, and when the flowers start to appear, cut the leaves and hang them up to dry for winter use.

CATNIP, or catmint, is a pretty border plant that attracts bees and cats. Old-fashioned beekeepers would often rub some around the inside of hives to welcome in a new swarm. Cats love this plant and will roll on it trying to cover themselves in its scent. Catnip does contain nepetalactone, which is an insect repellant.

Rosemary, 'it is the herb sacred to remembrance and therefore, to friendship'

SIR THOMAS MOORE

A sprig of savory, rubbed onto a wasp or bee sting, brings instant relief.

Savory repels blackfly and so makes a good companion to susceptible plants.

BORAGE takes its name from the Celtic word *borrach* meaning 'to have courage'. Its Welsh name is *Llawenlys* – herb of gladness. Borage has always enjoyed a reputation for bringing happiness and courage to those that eat it. It produces lovely sky-blue flowers and the whole plant has the scent of cucumber. Both leaves and flowers are added to cooling summer drinks.

How to make
CANDIED ANGELICA
angelica stems
4oz/25g salt
1½lb/750g granulated sugar
4oz/125g caster sugar

Cut the angelica stems into 4 inch/10cm pieces, pour over 1 pint/600ml hot water in which the salt has been dissolved. Cover and leave for twenty four hours. Drain, peel and wash the stems well in cold water. Make a syrup of 1½ pints/900ml water and the granulated sugar and simmer gently for ten minutes. Using a slotted spoon lower the angelica pieces into the boiling syrup, boil for twenty minutes. Lift out and drain. Put in a cool oven 175°F/70°C/Gas Mark ¼ for at least one hour to dry completely. Dredge with caster sugar and store in an airtight jar.

ANGELICA was one of the foremost medicinal plants. It was considered a good remedy for coughs, colds, lung disorders, colic and rheumatism. The whole plant, roots and all, is aromatic. In his *Callender for Gardening* of 1661, Stevenson writes 'be sure every morning to perfume your house with angelica seeds, burnt in a fire-pan or chafing dish of coals'. You may recognise the aroma in Vermouth and Chartreuse. June is the time to cut the stems into strips and candy them for use as a decoration for puddings and cakes.

Sow borage, sow courage.

FORTUNE TELLING

A toddler should be taken into the herb garden and put amongst the herbs. The first plant he or she touches will foretell the future. If the child touches rue, then the future will be unhappy. Rosemary foretells a life of great contentment, thyme denotes a single life and sage, a life devoted to wisdom.

CONTROLLING PESTS

This is a time when your garden is particularly susceptible to attack from pests and diseases. Here are some ways Old Wives have dealt with them for centuries.

An effective way to deter slugs is to border vegetable beds with slates, smearing them with a paste of engine oil and soot.

If troubled by rabbits, protect your crops with a row of onions, chives, garlic or more elegantly with ornamental onions. Rabbits will never pass through such a border.

A sure deterrent for mice is to wash your cat and sprinkle the water over the garden!

Tie sacking around the trunks of apple and pear trees to catch apple blossom weevils.

To protect cucumbers from wireworm, push a fresh carrot into the soil near each plant.

Lengths of black thread tied around fruit bushes will protect them from birds.

Stamp on a lupin, then smear the crushed flower around the trunk of a fruit tree and ants will never climb up it.

A mulch of oak leaves will repel slugs and snails.

Rosa alba

JULY

The kiss of the sun for pardon,
The song of the birds for mirth
One is nearer God's heart in a garden
Than anywhere else on earth.

DOROTHY FRANCES GURNEY

This month is distinguished by its high range of
temperature and is remarkable for the
variability of the rainfull: usually we have dry
weather during the first half and a spell of wet weather
in the second, the break occuring about
St. Swithin's Day.

THE GARDEN ORACLE, 1896

The English winter
– ending in July to recommence
in August.
LORD BYRON

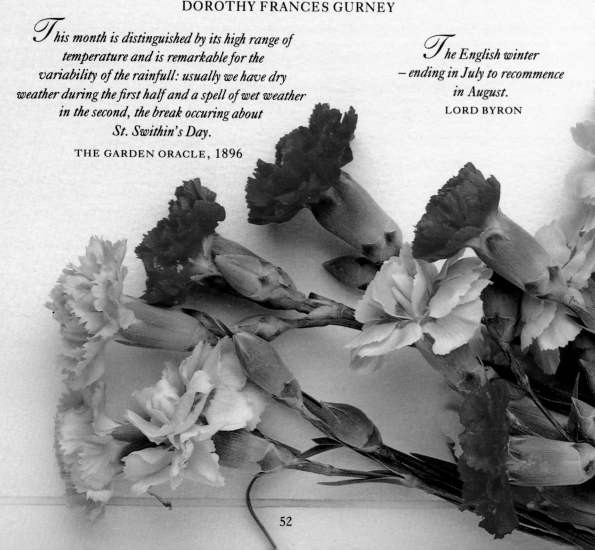

THE FLOWER GARDEN

Carnation

CARNATIONS and their close relations, pinks, have been popular garden plants for centuries. They were particularly favoured in Tudor knot gardens, and some of the old varieties are still available: *Raby Castle* is a salmon pink colour and was a Victorian favourite, *Oakfield Clove* is of a deep crimson hue with a pronounced scent of cloves, and *Fenbow's Nutmeg Clove* is one of the oldest carnations in cultivation.

Carnations have long been associated with weddings and their clove-scented flowers were once used to spice wine given to brides after the wedding ceremony. They were believed to be an aphrodisiac, indeed in Italy to this day the carnation is a symbol of ardent love. The ancient Greeks held the plant in great esteem and used the flower extensively in garlands and coronets, from whence came its early name, coronation.

*Bring carnations and sops
in wine worn of paramours*

EDMUND SPENSER

SWEET WILLIAM is from the same family as the carnation and the pink. The origin of its name is unclear – it certainly grew wild in Normandy so it may refer to William the Conqueror or perhaps it commemorates William of Aquitaine and owes its presence on our shores to his followers, the Carthusian monks.

'These plants are not used either in mete or medicine but esteemed for their beauty, to deck up gardens and the bosoms of the beautiful' wrote John Gerard in his famous Herbal, published in 1597.

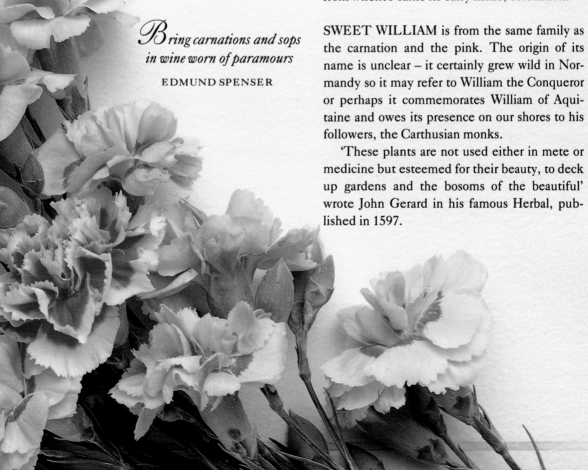

Pour beer dregs over your hollyhocks and they will grow tall and strong.

THE HYDRANGEA is a deciduous shrub with flowers of either blue or pink, depending on the chemical make-up of the soil in which it grows. In Devon, Victorian gardeners used to call the hydrangea 'changeables' for this very reason. Blue flowers were considered the most desirable, and it was common practice to grind up blue slates and fork this dust into the soil around each bush.

THE HOLLYHOCK was brought to this country from China. It was much prized as a medicinal plant to soothe coughs and diseases of the lungs, and a poultice of the leaves is said to relieve wasp and bee stings. The dried and powdered flowers make a wonderful natural dye – a lovely deep purplish-black.

MORNING GLORY to some, bindweed to others, this member of the convolvulus family will strangle any plants near it if left to run riot. Its pretty flowers open with the sunshine and close during dull weather, at the approach of rain and at night. The flowers have been used as a symbol of the transience of man's life: they open in the morning, are in full flower by midday, and fade in the evening.

It was a plant favoured by witches, who believe their magic to be particularly strong if plucked three days before the full moon. Children are warned not to pick the flowers because all parts of the plant are believed to be poisonous – it contains a chemical which can cause hallucinations.

Bindweed, unlike other climbing plants, grows contrary to the sun. If the plant is forced to grow in the other direction and trapped so that it cannot disengage itself, it will perish.

THE WATER LILY, according to Culpeper, is governed by the moon and is therefore a plant that will cool and moisten. The leaves were used to reduce fevers and the syrup of the flowers induced sleep and calmed distracted patients.

Some varieties can be grown in just a few inches of water, others need a depth of up to five feet. All produce impressive flowers which, unfortunately, only last for four or five days.

Place hollyhock flowers round the edges of a room to repel lice and fleas.

Plant hollyhocks next to beehives, as the nectar makes beautiful honey.

SNAPDRAGONS grow wild on old stone walls and chalky cliffs. In Tudor times the plant was prized as a charm against witchcraft. Country names such as toad mouth or lion mouth come from the children's game of squeezing the sides of the blossom, causing the petals to open like a mouth.

If weeds are a problem in gravel paths, water with a mixture of salt, ashes and tobacco sweepings.

NIGHT-SCENTED STOCK is a variety of wallflower. It was used by the Elizabethans to ease the pains of childbirth, for paralysis and piles. The stock has grown wild in this country for many centuries and the heady perfume which it exudes in the early evening is well-loved in cottage gardens.

Those anointed with the oil of snapdragon seeds are believed to be destined for fame.

A JULY CALENDAR

1st July

If the first of July be rainy weather
'Twill rain, more or less, for four weeks together.

3rd July

THE DOG DAYS begin now and last till August 11th. Linked with the rising of the Dog Star, Sirius, these are the hottest and unhealthiest days of the year.

St. Swithin's Day, if thou dost rain
For forty days it will remain.
St. Swithin's Day, if thou be fair
For forty days, 'twill rain no mair.
MIDLANDS WEATHER RHYME

15th July
ST SWITHIN'S DAY

St. Swithin is closely associated with the weather and the ripening of apples. His remains were moved on this day in 971 AD from their original humble resting place to Winchester Cathedral. According to legend, the saint so resented being disturbed that he began to weep, causing heavy rain to fall for the next forty days.

A light shower on St. Swithin's day was said to be the Saint christening the apples, and in many rural areas no-one would eat an apple until after this day.

20th July
ST. MARGARET'S DAY

St. Margaret is the patron saint of safe childbirth and for some reason her feast day was considered the right day to plant turnips.

22nd July
FEAST OF ST. MARY MAGDALENE

Heavy rain at this time of the month can be devastating for the harvest and the garden, hence the rhyme:

A Magdalene flood
Never did good.

'Til St. Swithin's day be past,
The apples be not fit to taste.

HUNTINGDONSHIRE SAYING

Seashore Flowers

THE SEA PINK, also known as thrift, is perhaps the commonest and most attractive of seaside plants. Its foliage forms soft green hummocks from which pink flowers rise on leafless stems. This pretty wild flower, which can be grown in the garden from seed, attracts both bees and butterflies.

SEA CAMPION grows wild on cliffs and in cultivated form in rock gardens. Its non-flowering stems lie flat on the ground and delicate white flowers appear on stalks up to 6 inches/15cm high.

SEA LAVENDER grows on long stalks in marshy ground and its flowers, while not smelling as strongly as English lavender, are nonetheless attractive to bees and provide an excellent source of nectar.

GORSE is a sturdy, stunted shrub that thrives particularly well near the sea. It flowers practically all year round. The golden yellow blooms have a powerful, buttery smell and yield a beautifully coloured dye. Gorse is often burned down. Its ashes are rich in alkali which is a wonderful natural fertilizer. In the 19th century it was commonly used as fuel in bakers' ovens.

*When gorse is not in bloom,
kissing is out of season.*

*Small pieces of gorse, put into
the drills when planting peas,
provide a good defence against
birds and mice.*

THE VEGETABLE GARDEN

THE GLOBE ARTICHOKE is one of the world's oldest cultivated vegetables. The Greeks and Romans were very fond of it and the Elizabethans grew it both as a vegetable and an ornamental plant. Culpeper and others believed this vegetable to be ruled by Venus and 'to provoke lust'.

Only the immature flower heads are eaten, so pick when very young.

THE TOMATO was brought to this country from South America in the 16th century. Regarded initially as an ornamental climber and somewhat of a curiosity, it failed – in spite of its reputation as a strong aphrodisiac – to gain much popularity until Victorian times. The plant's close resemblance to deadly nightshade – they are part of the same family – probably had something to do with a general reluctance to eat the succulent red fruits.

THE CUCUMBER appeared on the table of the Roman Emperor Tiberius daily, winter and summer. It was considered a great luxury, along with the melon. Here in Britain gardeners considered that old seed produced better fruit than new, and so would age new seed by carrying it around in their waistcoat pockets before planting it.

The cucumber was believed to grow in direct response to the virility of the sower, and should therefore be planted by a young, naked man. Cucumbers planted by women, children and old men would not thrive.

It is a cool and soothing salad vegetable, and it is also cooling, soothing and beautifying to the skin.

How to make
CUCUMBER SUNBURN LOTION

Peel and dice two large cucumbers, place in the top of a double boiler, cover lightly and cook gently until soft. Squeeze the cooked cucumber through fine muslin. Add to the juice one quarter of its volume of whisky and one-third of elder-flower water. Shake well and bottle.

*Plant your seeds in a row,
One for the pheasant, one for the crow,
One to rot and one to grow.*

THE LETTUCE has been cultivated for centuries. The Egyptians grew them and dedicated them to their goddess of increase, Min. Lettuces were widely believed to have magical powers and healing properties. The Romans ate them at banquets to counteract the effects of wine and in medieval times they were used in love potions and to promote child-bearing, but their most common medicinal use was to induce sleep.

John Evelyn, who wrote his *Discourse of Sallets* in 1699, believed that the eating of lettuce would uphold morals, temperance and chastity, but considering that the active constituent in the wild lettuce resembles a mild opium, it seems unlikely.

A thick sowing of turnip seed will rid the land of couch grass.

Grow marigolds near your tomato plants to keep pests at bay.

Cut thistles in May
They grow in a day;
Cut them in June,
That is too soon;
Cut them in July,
Then they die.

THE HERB GARDEN

BASIL, a wonderfully fragrant and aromatic herb, is a native of India and therefore prefers sunshine. In India, the basil plant is considered sacred to Krishna and Vishnu and is venerated in every Hindu home.

To the ancient Greeks it represented hate and misfortune, in fact poverty was depicted as a woman in rags with a basil plant at her side. Both the Greeks and Romans thought that the plant would not grow unless it was verbally abused and sworn at while the seeds were being sown.

In Persia, Egypt and Malaysia basil is planted on graves, and in Italy it is considered a love-token. In Elizabethan times, farmers' wives would give little pots of basil to their guests as a token of friendship.

PARSLEY is such a popular herb, it is curious that it has such an unlucky reputation in folk lore. In ancient Greece and Rome it was associated with death – graves were strewn with it. As it was the Romans who brought parsley to Britain, our beliefs surrounding this herb have probably sprung from theirs.

It is hard to know where to begin the catalogue of parsley lore. Parsley plants should never be given away, as if you give away parsley you give away your luck, although it is all right to let someone steal it. Parsley must never be transplanted, it is better to destroy it and start again. In order to thrive parsley must be sown only by a woman; only on Good Friday; only when church bells are ringing and if sown by a woman of childbearing years, the woman will be pregnant by the time the seeds germinate. Parsley was considered to be an antidote to poison and to put it on food was a sign of goodwill.

A certain Gentleman of Siena being wonderfully taken and delighted with the Smell of Basil, was wont very frequently to take the Powder of the dry Herb and Stuff it up his Nose; but in a short time he turn'd mad and died; and his Head being opened by Surgeons, there was found a Nest of Scorpions in the Brain.

TOURNEFORT, *THE COMPLEAT HERBAL*

SUMMER FAIRS

July is a popular time for fairs, some of which are directly associated with particular fruits that ripen at this time of year. The origins of most fairs are tied up with religious festivals and the church calendar. Over the centuries, the religious element has often been forgotten and fairs have been associated with selling produce and having fun. In the days when only large towns had shops, the fair was a chance to catch up on gossip, meet old friends and to buy local produce which was in abundance. The Black Cherry fair is held on the second Saturday in July at Chertsey in Surrey. Later in the month, the Wisbech Strawberry Fair is one of the many Strawberry Fairs held up and down the country from the middle to the end of July.

Dig in chopped green bracken when planting fuschia to encourage the roots to grow.

LADYBIRDS

Apart from doing an excellent job of keeping aphids numbers down, the ladybird is also a sign of good fortune. The deeper red the ladybird, the better the luck, and in some areas the number of spots means the number of happy months in a year.

If one alights on you, do not brush it off, wait for it to fly away of its own accord. To help it on its way you can blow on it and recite the well known rhyme:

Ladybird, ladybird, fly away home,
Your house in on fire, your children are gone.
Except just one and that's little Joan
And she crept under the frying pan.

THE FRUIT GARDEN

CHERRIES are starting to ripen now, providing the birds haven't eaten them all. The only way to save some for yourself is to throw a net over the whole tree. Some of the best eating varieties include the *Merton Bigarreau*, an almost black cherry with a superb flavour; *Merton Bounty*, which has dark, crimson fruit and the *Merton Favourite*, a heart-shaped, dark, sweet cherry.

Cherry ripe, cherry ripe,
Ripe I cry,
Full and fair ones,
Come and buy.

TRADITIONAL STREET CRY

RASPBERRIES grow best where the summer days are long and cool. Indeed the best raspberries in the world are grown in Scotland, where the climate suits the fruit perfectly. Those varieties with yellow fruit are said to be the most tasty. Should rain fall on the ripe fruits, pick them immediately after the rain has stopped. Bottle or freeze what you can't eat raw, left only for a short time mould will develop and spread rapidly.

GOOSEBERRIES are native to Northern Europe, and the taste for them has never really spread to the south. In Britain and in the Scandinavian countries gooseberries are popular in tarts, jams and sauces to accompany oily fish. Yellow gooseberries have the best flavour and they make an excellent sparkling wine.

Do not let raspberries fruit in their first year, or the plant will be seriously weakened.

How to make
GOOSEBERRY CHAMPAGNE

'To every Scotch pint (2 quarts) of gooseberries mashed, add 1½ quarts of water, and 12 ounces of good loaf sugar bruised and dissolved. Stir the whole well in the tub or vat, and throw a blanket over the vessel; which is proper in making all wines, unless you wish to slacken the process of fermentation. Stir the ingredients occasionally; and in three days strain off the liquor into a cask. Keep the cask full, and when the spiritous fermentation has ceased, add for every gallon of wine ½ pint of brandy or good whisky, and the same quantity of Sherry or Madeira. Bung up the cask very closely, covering the bung with clay; and when fined, which will be in from three to six months, rack it carefully off.'

FROM THE COOK AND
HOUSEWIFE'S MANUAL
BY MEG DODS, 1826

Gooseberries provoke the appetite and coole the vehement heate of the stomache and liver.

JOHN GERARD

To harvest gooseberries: Wearing a thick leather glove, strip off the fruit by pulling a branch through the hand, letting the fruit fall onto a sheet.

AUGUST

Sing a song of seasons!
Something bright in all!
Flowers in the Summer
Fires in the Fall.

R. L. STEVENSON

The best top dressing for lilies is wood ash.

If lilies are plentiful, bread will be cheap.

Very hot weather in the first week of August presages a hard winter.

THE FLOWER GARDEN

Lily

WHILST THE ROSE is probably the flower most praised in prose and poetry, the white lily, commonly called the Madonna lily, is the most painted, certainly by the old masters. It has been cultivated for some 3,500 years and was adopted by the Christian church in its early days as a symbol of purity. It is a native of the Mediterranean and is believed to have been brought here by the Crusaders. It is a flower much associated with weddings and funerals and has a strong, sweet scent which can be oppressive in a small room.

The presence of lilies in a house was once believed to surround the occupants with an aura of holiness and give protection against witchcraft and other evils. In the garden lilies would only grow well for a good woman. The lily did have a more practical use – an ointment made from the ground roots was, apparently, an effective cure for boils and burns.

Other varieties of lily that are popular in the cottage garden include *The Scarlet Turk's Cap Lily*, a popular plant in Tudor times, with scarlet leaves and red stamens; *The Martagon Lily*, which has up to twenty drooping flowers on each stalk and *The Tiger Lily*, which reached Britain in the 19th century and has grown as a food plant in China for 2000 years.

To gild refined gold, to paint the Lily,
To throw a perfume on the Violet . . .
Is wasteful and ridiculous.

W. SHAKESPEARE

A lily root does not like to be
disturbed, so never move them,
just replace them as they loose their
strength.

HONEYSUCKLE, also called woodbine, is a climbing plant that will twine itself around anything in its path. It has a wonderful scent which is particularly strong and attractive at nightfall as it relies on the nocturnal moth for pollination.

THE DELPHINIUM is a well-loved cottage garden plant which owes its name to the shape of its flowers, seen as resembling a dolphin's nose (delphinium comes from the Greek word for dolphin). It is a perennial which will flower year after year without needing much assistance from the gardener. Children should be warned against putting any part of this plant into their mouths as it contains an irritant poison called delphanine. A tincture made from these seeds is traditionally used to destroy hair lice.

Add a spoonful of sugar to the water in which cut delphiniums are arranged and they will last longer.

Plant honeysuckle with its roots in the shade and its flowers in the sun.

THE POPPY is the flower of sleep and oblivion. According to Greek legend, it was created by Somnus, the god of sleep, to help Ceres, the corn goddess, who was so exhausted by the search for her lost daughter that she couldn't make the corn grow. The poppies soothed her to sleep and when she had rested, the corn grew again, giving rise to the belief that the presence of poppies was essential for the welfare of the corn.

Poppy seeds can lie dormant for many years and will germinate when the soil is disturbed. This is what happened on the battlefields of Flanders where the digging of the trenches caused the poppies to bloom and since the First World War the poppy has become a symbol of remembrance for those killed in war.

To stare too long at wild poppies is supposed to cause blindness – hence local names such as blind eyes and blindy buffs.

Pleasures are like poppies spread, You seize the flow'r, its bloom is shed.
ROBERT BURNS

GLADIOLI are thought to be the 'lilies of the field' mentioned by Christ in the Sermon on the Mount, as these flowers grew in great profusion in the Holy Land at that time. They were introduced into this country by John Tradescant, gardener to Charles I. Also known as the sword lily, this dramatic plant was a favourite in Victorian and Edwardian gardens. According to the herbalist John Gerard, a poultice made from the corm of the gladiolus was good for drawing out splinters.

THE SUNFLOWER was worshipped by the Peruvian Incas as a symbol of the sun. Their priestesses wore golden medallions fashioned in its image. It was introduced to this country in the 16th century, and became a popular feature in city gardens because the sunflower is happy in smog, fog and polluted air, where more tender blooms would perish.

As the sunflower turns to her god when he sets The same look which she turn'd when he rose.
MOORE'S IRISH MELODIES

*F*ADING ROSES

As summer draws to a close, rose petals start to fall. Gather them on a warm, dry morning, just before they fall. Spread petals on sheets of paper and leave in a warm, dry place for several days, turning regularly.

How to make
ROSE PETAL POT-POURRI

3 cups dried rose petals
2 cups dried lavender flowers
1 cup dried lemon verbena leaves
1 tablespoon powdered allspice
1 tablespoon cinnamon
1 tablespoon ground cloves
¹/₄oz/5g gum benzoin

Mix together all the dry ingredients and add the gum benzoin. Stir well. Put into a screw-topped jar and store in a warm place for two weeks. Shake regularly. When required turn out into a dish or bowl and enjoy the perfumes of summer.

THE PASSION FLOWER is so called because of its supposed resemblance to Christ's Crown of Thorns. Priests in Brazil, from whence the plant originates, believed that its profusion of climbing flowers symbolised the conversion of local Indians to Christianity. Early discoverers of this lush, exotic bloom attributed all its parts to representations of the crucifixion. The leaves were said to represent the spear; the five anthers, the five wounds; the tendrils, the whips; the central column, the pillar of the cross; the three styles, the three nails; the threads within the flowers, the crown of thorns and the calyx, the 'Glory'. Added to this, the flower was said to remain open for three days to symbolise the three years of Christ's ministry, but in fact the beautiful passion flower remains open for only one day.

*P*lant *parsley next to roses to*
increase their scent.

THE HIBISCUS is a native of Africa and was brought to this country in the 16th century. In the South Sea Islands a red hibiscus blossom behind a girl's left ear means 'I desire a lover'; behind her right ear it means 'I already have a lover'. A flower behind each ear, however, conveys the daring message 'I have a lover, but would like another'.

THE NASTURTIUM is said to have sprung from the blood of a Trojan warrior. The blossom symbolised his golden helmet and the round leaf his shield. It is a close relation to watercress, which explains why its leaves make such a tasty addition to salads. The seeds of this creeping, twining plant, when pickled, make a good substitute for capers.

Ah beauteous flower! whose centre glows
With studs of gold; thence streaming flows
Ray-like effulgence; next is seen
A rich expanse of varying hue,
Enfring'd with an empurpled blue
And streak'd with young Pomana's green.
ANON, THE PASSION FLOWER

Water in which parings from
horse's hooves have been soaked
makes a good fertilizer for roses.

THE HERB GARDEN

CHAMOMILE (*Chamaemelum nobile*) is one of the oldest herbs known to man. The origin of its name is Greek, meaning ground apple. As its name suggest it is a low, creeping plant that gives off a definite apple scent. It was often used on walkways as its perfume is very pronounced when trodden underfoot.

It is believed to be a good garden tonic, chamomile plants dotted around the garden will improve the lustre of the plants around them. Chamomile is a popular infusion, recommended as a general tonic and also a sedative good for restless children and those who have trouble sleeping.

Like a chamomile bed –
The more it is trodden,
The more it will spread.

How to make
CHAMOMILE HAIR RINSE
2oz/50g wild chamomile flowers
2 pints/1 litre boiling water

Put the chamomile flowers into a jug and pour over the boiling water. Leave to infuse for 20 minutes, before straining. Wash the hair and use the infusion as a final rinse, pouring it through the hair several times.

This hair rinse is considered particularly suitable for blonde hair. Rosemary leaves, treated in the same way, will improve dark hair of all types.

Chamomile Harvest.

LAVENDER owes its name to the Latin word 'lavare' – to wash – a reference to its use in scenting water for bathing. It is cultivated for its fragrance and English lavender is the variety most sought after in the perfumery business. Bunches of dried lavender give off a lovely scent, and the dried, crushed flowers are used in pot-pourri and for sachets.

Sachets of lavender stored with linen will perfume it and keep the cupboards free of moths and other insects.

If lavender grows well in the garden, the girls of the house will never marry.

How to make
A LAVENDER SWEET BAG

4 cups dried lavender flowers
4 cups dried rose petals
2 cups dried thyme
2 cups dried lemon thyme
2 cups dried eau-de-cologne mint
2 cups dried marjoram
1/3 cup ground cloves
2 cups dried orris root

In a large bowl mix all the ingredients together and put into small muslin or silk bags. Tie with a narrow satin or velvet ribbon. If the bag is to be a gift, decorate with scraps of lace and tiny dried rosebuds.

These 'sweet bags' can be pinned to cushions and chair backs to scent the room, as was popular in Victorian times.

Lavender oil is an effective cure for lice and worms in cats and dogs.

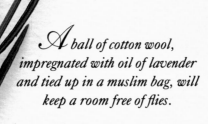

A ball of cotton wool, impregnated with oil of lavender and tied up in a muslin bag, will keep a room free of flies.

THE VEGETABLE GARDEN

ONIONS were once widely believed to ward off infection. During the plague epidemics that swept Europe in the 15th, 16th and 17th centuries, it was recommended that three or four peeled onions should be left on the ground for ten days to fight the infection. The strong fumes were supposed to kill infection but as an additional benefit they would deter snakes.

The onion also has curative powers. A popular remedy for chilblains was to rub the affected area with a piece of onion and some salt. For baldness the old herbals recommended rubbing the bald patch with an onion until the skin was quite red, then smearing it thickly with honey.

CELERY arrived in this country at the time of Elizabeth I, when it was used both as a herbal tonic and a salad vegetable. Although the stalk is the most commonly eaten part, the tops are full of vitamins and can be used to good advantage in soups and stews.

BEES AND BEEKEEPING

Bees are supposed to be the wisest of insects, and many superstitions are associated with them. Bees should never be killed, nor should they be sold as a bought swarm will never thrive – however they can be bartered in exchange for goods. If you own a hive and someone in the family dies or marries, you must go and tell the bees or they will desert the hive, if they continue to hum, they have accepted the news.

If your house is rent with arguments and swearing, your bees will not thrive.

An AUGUST CALENDAR

1st August
LAMMAS DAY

In Medieval times, Lammas Day marked the beginning of the harvest. Traditionally a loaf of bread would be baked using the first cutting of corn and the load would be taken to church on this day to be blessed by the priest.

24th August
ST. BARTHOLOMEW'S DAY

St. Bartholomew is the patron saint of butchers and tanners and beekeepers. His feast day was celebrated with great fairs. As the season's apple and pear crop were just ripening, these fruits played a great part in the proceedings.

St. Bartholomew is supposed to bring the 'cold dew', the cooler autumn weather, and it is his day that ends the forty days of rain promised by a wet St. Swithin's Day.
If Bartlemas Day be fine and clear
You may hope for a prosperous autumn this year.

29th August
ST JOHN THE BAPTIST'S DAY

This day commemorates the anniversary of the death of St John. It is on this day that St John's wort, the saint's special herb, is said to show spots of red upon its leaves.

All the tears St. Swithin can cry
St. Barthelmy's mantle can wipe dry.

THE FRUIT GARDEN

Harvest fruits as they ripen and protect those that are still on the bush or tree from birds and wasps. Soft fruits such as plums are a magnet to wasps, so hang jars containing beer dregs and sugar in the branches of fruit trees and the wasps will fly in and drown.

GREENGAGES are considered the finest of all eating plums. They were brought to England from France by Sir William Gage in 1724. In France they are highly-prized, and called Reine-Claude after the wife of Francis I, who grew these plums at their castle in the Loire Valley – an area now overrun with greengages. The best British varieties are those developed by Jervaise Coe around 1800 – Coe's Golden Drop is reputed to be his best.

DAMSON trees grow to a fair size, but will not start to fruit until they are at least five years old. It is said that the fruiting of the damson tree runs in three year cycles – a heavy crop, a poor crop and an average crop following each other in rotation. In heavy cropping years you may have to support the branches with wooden posts.

THE VICTORIA PLUM is the best known of plums and is widely grown in cottage gardens. It is regarded as a dessert plum, but in truth it is a cooking plum, excellent for jam-making and tarts. Plums are ripe for picking as soon as a bloom appears on the skin, do not wait until they are soft.

MODERN
FRUIT GROWING

BY
W. P. SEABROOK
OF
SEABROOK & SONS, LTD., THE NURSERIES, CHELMSFORD

How to make
DAMSON CHEESE
2lb/1 kilo damsons
1lb/¹/₂ kilo granulated sugar per
1lb/¹/₂ kilo damson purée

Heat the oven to 325°F/160°C/Gas Mark 3. Wash the damsons and put them into an earthenware casserole dish with a tight-fitting lid. Cook until the juices run freely and the stones are loose – approximately 30 minutes. Put the mixture through a fine sieve. Crack the stones, take out the kernels and put these through the sieve also. Measure the purée and granulated sugar, pound for pound. Put both into a saucepan and boil until setting point is reached. Pour into clean, dry jars and seal as for jam.

This preserve, which is one of the oldest country recipes, should be kept for at least six months before using. It can be served, decorated with toasted almonds and doused in port, as an elegant dessert.

Plant nasturtiums around your fruit trees and encourage the flowers to twist up the trunk. They will repel troublesome insects and encourage fruitfulness.

If you keep chickens, let them run about under your plum trees, their droppings make rich manure.

How to make
PLUMS INTO PRUNES
A quantity of fresh, ripe plums

Wash the fruit well and put into a large bowl. Pour over boiling water to cover and leave for one minute. Drain and plunge into cold water. Drain again and dry thoroughly. Place on a perforated tray and dry in a pre-heated oven, 140°F/70°C/Gas Mark ¹/₄, leaving the oven door slightly open, turning occasionally.

SEPTEMBER

The Michaelmas Daisies, among dead weeds,
Blooms for St. Michael's valorous deeds
And seems the last of flowers that stood
Till the feast of St. Simon and St. Jude.

ANON

Evening red and morning grey
Are the sure signs of a fine day

September blow soft
'Til the fruit's in the loft.

THOMAS TUSSER

THE FLOWER GARDEN

Michaelmas Daisy

THE MICHAELMAS DAISY is part of the huge aster family, and is so called because it blooms around Michaelmas, 29th September. It is a native of America and was discovered by the Belgian Botanist, Hermann.

In ancient Greece and Rome, the wild aster was considered sacred and many myths surround this daisy-like plant. It was believed that the goddess Asterea, looking down upon earth, saw no stars. So distressed was she by this that she started to cry, and asters burst into bloom, watered by her tears. Another charming legend tells of the gods scattering stardust on the earth, and thereafter asters blossomed in the fields.

Victorian apiarists planted asters near their beehives to improve the quality of their honey.

In the Language of Flowers, all species of crocus represent good cheer.

THE ACANTHUS is an elegant plant which was introduced into Britain from Italy during the Middle Ages. It was widely used in medicine at one time, and was said to cure gout and soothe burns and scalds.

The acanthus leaf has been the inspiration for many decorative designs, particularly during the Arts and Crafts period – it was a favourite motif of William Morris. It is claimed that the acanthus leaf inspired the Greek architect Callimachus in the design of the columns for a temple at Corinth.

THE SAFFRON CROCUS is the true crocus; the plant that gave its name to Saffron Walden where it was once much cultivated. It is the stigma of this species (not the poisonous autumn crocus) that are used to make saffron, the costly, fragrant yellow spice, used today for colouring and flavouring a variety of dishes. Saffron has always been an expensive substance. It has been estimated that 60,000 stigmas are required to make just one pound of this precious spice.

An infusion of garlic, used as a spray, will repel aphids and scale insects and prevent mildew in cucumbers, rust in beans and blight in tomatoes.

Plant crocuses near a lavender hedge and the birds will not pull the flowers to pieces.

THE AUTUMN CROCUS was known descriptively to country folk as upstarts, naked ladies, or star-naked boys. All these names refer to the fact that the blooms appear without the leaves. Another, earlier name was *filius ante patrem* which translates as 'the son before the father'. It was so called because it was thought that the late-flowering plant gave its seeds before its flowers; in fact the seeds follow in spring.

It is a poisonous plant. In ancient Greece, slaves were known to eat small quantities of the bulb in order to get time off work. They would become too sick for work but not dangerously so.

How to
DRY HYDRANGEA FLOWER HEADS

September is a good time for drying hydrangea flower heads. Wait until the flowers have begun to change colour and the stamens have withered, before cutting them from the bush. Place the flowers upright in a vase tall enough to support them. Pour in about 2in/10cm of water. When all this water has been used up, the flowers should be left to dry naturally.

The flower of the saffron doth rise out of the ground nakedly in September . . . it groweth plentifully in Cambridgeshire: at Saffron Walden and other places thereabouts, as corn in the field.

JOHN GERARD

*The South wind brings
wet weather;
The North wind
wet and cold together;
The West wind brings
us rain;
The East wind blows
it back again.*

FRED DOWSON,
1ST PRIZE WINNER
'HORSE & GROOM'
LEEK SHOW, 1916,
CASTLESIDE.

SEPTEMBER.

Work in the Vegetable G

...verworked and the idle
...ill be full of seeds blown
...en, and the first shower
...ce. All that we have to
...be kept down, for they
...ps in seed-beds and spoil
...very much tend to keep
...en, if they were away, it
...he benefit of all the proper
...p crops that may be cleared
...ettuce, and even thinnings of
...er.

...and now with Cabbage plants,
...he kitchen constant. 'Crowd-
...s overcrowding, and it is only
...e plants so close together that
...The usual rule in planting ou
...time of year is to allow a distan
...But we carry the crowding p
...worts and other mini
...arge dots being

Lettuces
but the suppl
sorts should
which a c
manure p
thinning
Cos is o
valuabl
enoug
early

thi
w

GOLDEN ROD is a native of Canada and the northern states of America. Flowering all through September, its distinctive yellow flower heads provide a lovely splash of colour.

It has always been thought of as a very magical plant. Indeed it was believed that where it grew a secret treasure lay buried, and if it were to grow by a house door, then the inhabitants could expect great good fortune. Used by those with the necessary skills, golden rod was believed to be a powerful divining rod with the power to pinpoint hidden springs of water.

HEATHER is a hardy evergreen that flowers in the late summer and early autumn and without which no rocky mountain landscape would be complete. There is a bewildering variety of heathers, ranging in colour from the deepest purple to the palest orange to the whitest of white. And it is the white heather that is supposed to bring luck to both the giver and the receiver.

To preserve heathers in flower arrangements, keep the stems away from water and they will last for weeks.

As Lady's Laces, Everlasting Peas,
True-Love-Lies-Bleeding with the Hearts-at-Ease;
And Golden Rods and Tansy running high,
That o'er the pale top smiled on passer-by:
Flowers in my time which everyone would praise,
Though thrown like weeds from gardens nowadays.

JOHN CLARE

*S*PIDERS

Many superstitions have been woven around the spider: if you find one crawling on your clothes, it is a sign that money is coming your way. To see a spider spinning its web means the gift of new clothes and if you kill a spider it will result in misfortune and rain.

The spider also features in many old remedies. For instance, a cure for whooping cough entails wearing a bag of live spiders around the neck. Those of nervous disposition were advised to make spider's webs into small pills which were then swallowed as tranquillizers and webs taken from cellars and outbuildings were used to staunch the flow of blood from small wounds.

The weather forecaster would do well to observe the spider. When a storm is approaching the spider will shorten the filaments from which his web is suspended, and when the calm returns he will let the threads out again.

Spiders often start to make their way into the warmth of the house in September, and it may be as well to remember the saying:

> If you wish to live and thrive,
> Let the spider run alive.

> *If violets bloom in the autumn,*
> *the person who owns the land will*
> *die.*

> *When black snails cross your path*
> *Black clouds much moisture hath.*

> *Fair weather first day*
> *of September*
> *Fair for the month.*

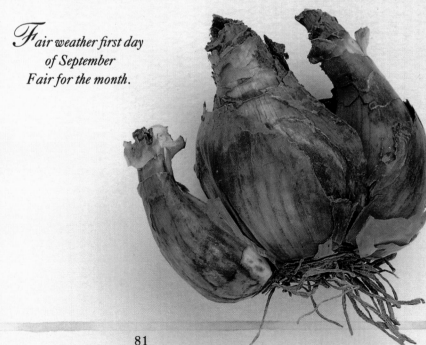

GENTIAN flowers are the most beautiful shade of blue. They are named after Gentius, a King of Illyria who reigned from 180 to 167 BC, and first recorded the medicinal values of these lovely plants. In England we enjoy it as a border plant, but in Germany and Switzerland they make schnapps from the root.

*Gentian wine was drunk
as an aperitif in the 18th century.*

A SEPTEMBER CALENDAR

14th September
DEVIL'S NUTTING DAY

Not a good day to visit your local nut trees, as it was once thought that if you should do so, the Devil would hold down the branches as you collected the crop.

The sky is as black at the Devil's
Nutting Bag
STAFFORDSHIRE WEATHER LORE,
PRESAGING A STORM

21st September
THE FEAST OF ST. MATTHEW

On the feast day of the patron saint of tax-gatherers, the evenings start to draw in and the temperature drops.

St Matthew
Brings cold rain and dew
But on the other hand:
Matthew's Day bright and clear
Brings good wine in next year

29th September
MICHAELMAS

This is the feast day of St. Michael the Archangel and one of the ancient quarter days – a time for paying rents and hiring servants. In many places Hiring or Mop Fairs would take place and Michaelmas Fairs are still part of country life.

Autumn is a good time for planting trees and in Victorian days it was believed that trees planted on this day would surely thrive:

A tree planted at Michaelmas
Will surely not go amiss!

HARVEST HOME

Before the Industrial Revolution, most people lived in the countryside and were dependent upon the food they produced themselves. Their very survival in winter depended on the success of the harvest. It is not surprising that the traditions of harvest time loom large even today.

The corn dolly is one such tradition. This was the last sheaf cut from the harvest. It was called the Harvest Queen or the Corn Dolly, although it had other names. In Devon they called it the Nek, in Wales the Hag, and in Yorkshire, Mell Doll. The sheaf was decorated with flowers and ribbons and taken home on the last waggon load with the cheering harvest workers. It was put in a prominent place whilst supper was eaten, a vast meal provided by the farm owner, and kept until replaced the following year when it would be ceremoniously burned and the ashes ploughed back into the soil.

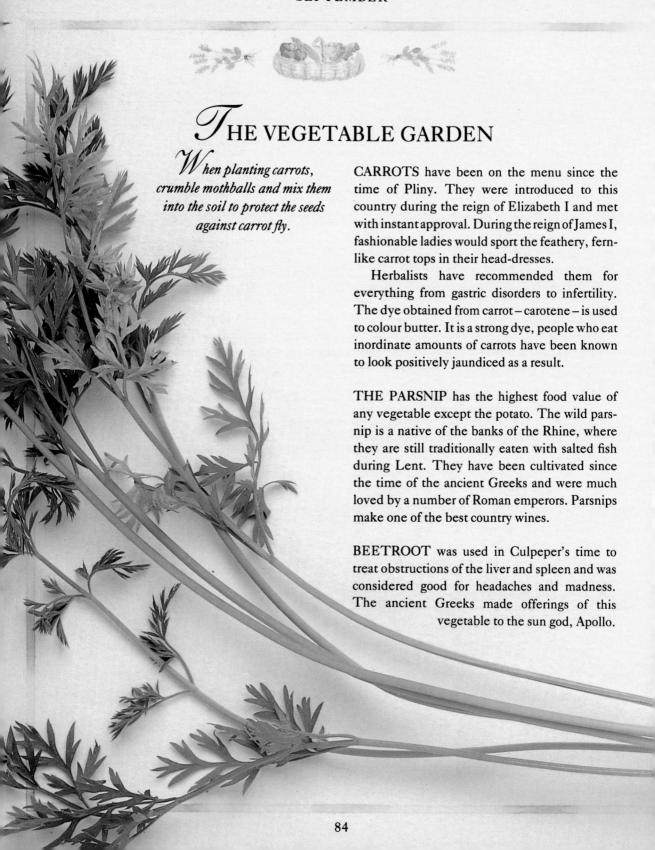

THE VEGETABLE GARDEN

When planting carrots, crumble mothballs and mix them into the soil to protect the seeds against carrot fly.

CARROTS have been on the menu since the time of Pliny. They were introduced to this country during the reign of Elizabeth I and met with instant approval. During the reign of James I, fashionable ladies would sport the feathery, fern-like carrot tops in their head-dresses.

Herbalists have recommended them for everything from gastric disorders to infertility. The dye obtained from carrot – carotene – is used to colour butter. It is a strong dye, people who eat inordinate amounts of carrots have been known to look positively jaundiced as a result.

THE PARSNIP has the highest food value of any vegetable except the potato. The wild parsnip is a native of the banks of the Rhine, where they are still traditionally eaten with salted fish during Lent. They have been cultivated since the time of the ancient Greeks and were much loved by a number of Roman emperors. Parsnips make one of the best country wines.

BEETROOT was used in Culpeper's time to treat obstructions of the liver and spleen and was considered good for headaches and madness. The ancient Greeks made offerings of this vegetable to the sun god, Apollo.

How to make
PARSNIP WINE

4lb/2 kilos parsnips
1lb/500g raisins
2½lb/1.1 kilos sugar
juice of 2 lemons
10fl oz/300ml freshly made strong tea
1tsp all-purpose wine yeast and nutrient
7 pints/4 litres water

Scrub the parsnips well and chop or mince finely. Put into a large saucepan with 6 pints/3.5 litres of water. Bring to the boil and simmer gently for 15 minutes. Skim off any scum that rises. Chop the raisins and put them into a plastic bucket with 1lb/500g sugar. Strain the hot parsnip water over them. Stir until the sugar has dissolved. Leave to cool and add the tea, lemon juice, yeast and nutrient. Cover tightly with a polythene sheet, and allow to ferment in a warm place for 7 days, stir daily. Strain through 4 thicknesses of muslin. Put the liquor back into the bucket and leave for a further 4 days. Pour into fermenting jars, leaving the sediment behind. Put the remaining sugar into a pan with 1 pint/½ litre of water and heat gently, stirring all the while. Allow to cool and add to fermenting jar. Fit air lock and leave until fermentation ceases. Rack and bottle. Keep for twelve months before drinking.

*Rowan tree and red thread
Haud the witches au' in dread*

SCOTTISH PROVERB

THE MAGIC ROWAN TREE

In Strathsey, a century ago, farmers would drive their cattle through a hoop of rowan, and then step through it themselves in order to guard themselves and their flock against evil. The rowan tree has long been associated with magic. Country people identified with this tree because of its hardiness and tenacity in cruel conditions. They hung branches of it on their houses and sheds and carried a small piece in their pockets for good luck. In times past, every Scottish croft would have had its rowan tree, so powerful was its magic considered to be.

If you have a rowan tree, you can make its magic work for you by tying a red ribbon onto it when the berries are out, and you will successfully keep witches from your home.

The berries are delicious in pies, jellies, jams and wine and needless to say rowan berries are a great temptation for the birds.

If you have lost your loved one, stick an apple with twelve new pins and place it in the fire. Call your lover's name and he or she is then obliged to appear.

APPLE TREES

Apples have always been a great favourite in Northern Europe. In Elizabethan times apples were served at the end of a feast with a little dish of caraway seeds to accompany them. Apple pies and puddings were as popular then as they are now, and cider a very popular drink.

The apple is one of the easiest foodstuffs to digest, and its unsweetened juice is known to reduce acidity in the stomach, thus aiding the whole digestive process. It is claimed that eating a ripe, juicy apple every day before bedtime will not only clean the teeth and massage the gums but also cure the worst cases of constipation.

In folklore apple remedies abound. Apple juice applied to the skin was thought to cure redness, and was often prescribed for red noses caused by drink. A cut apple rubbed onto warts and then buried in the garden was a common cure, as the apple rots in the ground, so the wart gradually disappears. Another belief was that the juice of an apple would help to heal small cuts, and modern research has shown that the pectin in the fruit does have germicidal qualities.

TRADITIONAL APPLE TREES

THE PITMASTON PINEAPPLE is an old variety of apple which is ready for picking in mid-September. This lovely apple was raised by Mr. White, steward to Lord Foley, around 1785. The fruit itself is small and conical. Although not commercially grown, it is an excellent garden variety for the apple connoisseur. Its flesh is yellow and firm and has a distinct pineapple flavour, juicy and sweet.

THE ST EDMUND'S RUSSET is a variety of russet apple that was developed at Bury St. Edmunds in Victorian times. It has a rough yellow skin and a good flavour and makes a fine garden tree.

To eat an apple going to bed
Will make the doctor beg his bread.

THE MAY QUEEN is one of the most attractive of apple trees. As its name suggest, it blossoms in May. It is only a small tree and is therefore most appropriate in a cottage garden. A good keeping apple, it has firm and juicy flesh.

THE CORNISH GILLYFLOWER is an apple variety that was found in a cottage garden near Truro and introduced by Sir Christopher Hawkins in 1813. It is a very high quality dessert apple with firm, fine-textured flesh and a rich, aromatic flavour.

THE COURT PENDU PLAT is thought to have been brought to this country by the Romans. It was first described in 1613. It is also known as the Wise Apple and is thought to be the original Forbidden Fruit plucked by Eve from the Tree of Knowledge.

How to
STORE APPLES FOR WINTER
Pick fruit for storing just before it is ripe. Russet varieties do not store well. Wrap each fruit separately in white tissue or newspaper. Pack them away in clean open boxes or trays and store in a cool, dry place. Maple leaves layered with the fruit will, it is said, help to preserve them.

OCTOBER

Pale amber sunlight falls across
The reddening October trees,
That hardly sway before a breeze,
As soft as summer: summer's loss
Seems little, dear, on days like these!

ERNEST DOWSON

Fall, leaves, fall; die, flowers, away;
Lengthen night and shorten day:
Every leaf speaks bliss to me
Fluttering from the autumn tree.

EMILY BRONTË,

THE FLOWER GARDEN
Marigold

THE ROMANS believed that the marigold, *Calendula officinalis*, to be a herb of the sun. At one time it was considered one of the most holy of plants by the Hindus, and garlands of these bright yellow flowers were hung around the necks of their gods.

In country areas of England, the marigold was known as 'husbandman's dial' because the flower head turns its face to sun as the day progresses, acting as a sort of primitive clock. Its other more common name, pot marigold, is a reference to its use in salads and soups, but beware – it has a reputation as a powerful aphrodisiac and apparently has the power to make one see fairies. The genus name *calends* reflects the fact that it seems to be in bloom every month of the year.

As a herb, the marigold was believed to cure jaundice, skin irritation and fever. A yellow dye extracted from the petals was once used in the dairy to colour cheese, and by the vain to colour their hair. Nowadays the petals are used cosmetically to cleanse and refresh oily skins.

The marigold is a cure-all in the garden. It exudes a substance that kills off bugs and whitefly, making it an ideal companion plant for just about everything, particularly tomatoes and potatoes.

In the decay of the moon,
A cloudy morning bodes a fair afternoon.

THE BLANKET FLOWER, called Galliarda in honour of the French botanist, Gaillard de Chantonnay, is a beautiful border plant that originates from North America and Mexico. It has an exceptionally long flowering period and provides a welcome splash of colour in the October garden.

THE ICE PLANT is a low, flowering evergreen, most at home in the rock garden. The Romans believed this plant would guard against lightening, and its Latin name, Sedum, comes from a word which means to calm or to allay.

There is a green variety, known as Lifelong, which flowers in the autumn and remains green for a long time after picking. Country maidens with cause to doubt their lovers would pick a sprig at Midsummer and pin it to the doorpost overnight. If in the morning it inclined to the right, the lover was true, but if to the left, he was not to be trusted.

Use the water from rinsing milk bottles for watering house plants – the much diluted milk substitutes for a mild liquid manure.

PHLOX comes from the Greek word meaning 'flame', an apt name for this bushy autumn-flowering shrub with unusually bright flowers. The flowers are very sweet-smelling and conjure up images of a Victorian country garden.

Phlox were extensively used in tussie-mussies and bouquets not only for their delightful perfume but because, to the Victorians, they were a symbol of sweet dreams and implied a proposal of marriage.

DREAM TIME

At this time of year dreams were thought to have special significance. To dream of flowers has a host of different meanings, depending upon the flowers that feature in your dreams.

Columbine suggests a happy adventure, cowslips signify unexpected luck and the crocus, a fresh start. Daffodils presage love and happiness, daisies a birth, holly a quarrel, lavender a reunion and harebells true love. To dream of a rose means that love is around the corner, but to dream of ivy warns that love will be clinging. Those who see visions of foxgloves in their sleep will be lucky in love, those who see marigolds will do well in life, and those who see lilies will do well to prepare for a life of solitude. The oak signifies good health, the pansy contentment and the mistletoe plant carries a wise message – a warning to be cautious in love.

How to make an
ELIZABETHAN TUSSIE-MUSSIE

Choose a perfect rose as the centrepiece of your bouquet. The red rose means 'love', while the musk rose means 'capricious beauty'. Surround it with lavender – 'silence', marigolds – 'happiness', forget-me-nots – 'faithfulness' and heliotrope – 'eternal love'. Marjoram and lily-of-the valley will convey a message of purity, happiness and humility. When your posy is completed, tie firmly with grosgrain ribbons in a variety of toning colours, which have previously been soaked in rosewater and dried. It should then be offered to the object of your affections! Flowers, dried and made into such a posy, will last for years. A few drops of a suitable essential oil can be shaken onto the flowers and the whole thing sealed away in a paper bag for a few months to 'cure'. Given to your loved one, it will then become a fairly permanent reminder of your affection.

AN OCTOBER CALENDAR

28th October
ST. SIMON AND ST. JUDE

In Medieval times, the weather on this day was taken as a measure for the next forty days. Expect the fine weather to break now, and winter gales to begin.

31st October
HALLOWE'EN

This is the Night of the Dead – the most unpredictable night of the year – and one on which festivals from many cultures collide.

Pomona, the Roman goddess of fruit trees, was hailed as an autumn diety, and her festival would certainly have been held around this time, hence its association with apples. It is the last day of the Celtic year – the day the Fairy Court rides out at midnight. In the Christian calendar this is the eve of the Feast of All Saints, when the dead in paradise are remembered.

On this magical night a girl wishing to see the face of her future husband should take an apple and a lighted candle into her darkened room. She should stand before the mirror and cut the apple into pieces. One piece should be thrown over the right shoulder and the other pieces eaten. All the time she should be combing her hair. At midnight, if she looks into the mirror she will see his image reflected there. On no account must she look behind her or she will conjure up all manner of evil spirits.

10th October
DEVIL'S BLACKBERRY DAY

From this day, according to folklore, blackberries are no longer safe to eat. It was widely believed that St. Michael the Archangel threw the Devil out of Heaven on October 9th. Falling to earth, the Devil landed in a blackberry bush and was so angered that he cursed the blackberries, making them unwholesome from this time on.

In the Midlands, the Devil was said to have thrown a veil over the blackberrry bushes on the 10th October. In fact, spider's webs start to be apparent on the bushes on damp, cold mornings, and it is true that at this time of year the berries begin to soften and attract insects. They do, therefore, become less wholesome from now on.

18th October
ST. LUKE'S DAY

The four days around St. Luke's Day used to be known as St. Luke's Little Summer – a spell of fine, clear weather ideal for planting winter wheat, cabbages and so forth.

Nuts and Nut Trees

HAZELNUTS are one of the most ancient of nuts. Also called filberts or cobs, they grow wild in the hedgerows. In Victorian times a bride would often be given a bag of hazelnuts as she left the church, usually by an older relative who already had children. This was offered as a token of fertility. A good crop of hazelnuts was said to foretell a larger number of births in the district than usual.

If you should find two nuts in a single shell, eat the one, make a wish and throw the other over your left shoulder. Your wish will be granted.

VICTORIAN RIDDLE:

I am within as white as snow,
Without as green as herbs that grow
I am higher than a house,
And yet am lesser than a mouse.

ANSWER:

A walnut hanging on a tree

THE WALNUT is a long-lived tree, large and handsome with strong branches. A native of - Persia (Iran), it is believed to have been brought to England by the Romans, who associated the tree with fertility. It was their custom to bury a gold coin amongst the roots as an offering to Pomona, goddess of fruit trees.

English walnuts are valued all over the world, and their lovely, old-fashioned names conjure up visions of old England even as you say them: Excelsior of Taynton, Franquette, Mayette, Northdown Clawnut, Patching Secrett.

Apart from being cracked open and eaten in front of a Christmas fire, walnuts are an essential ingredient in the kitchen. In fact one of the earliest recorded English recipe, c.1430, is for white fish with a walnut sauce. Walnut oil is light and flavoursome and particulary delicious in salads and was, incidently, used by painters to mix gold size, and by cabinetmakers to polish wood.

October hath always
One and twenty fine days

If the wind is in the west on the 12th October, a mild winter will follow.

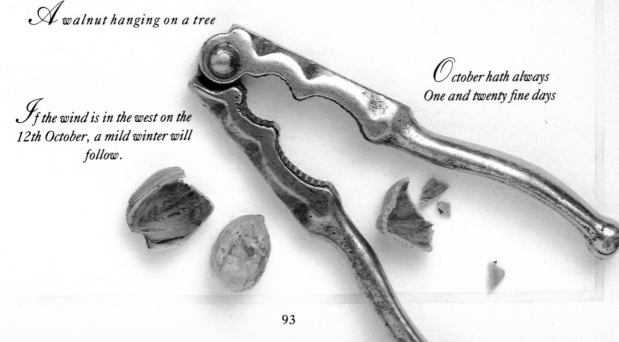

THE FRUIT GARDEN

THE QUINCE, almost orange in colour when ripe, is large and pear-shaped. It was believed by many country people to be the Forbidden Fruit of the Garden of Eden, but that superstition certainly did not stop them gathering quince and making sharp and flavourful jams, jellies and preserves. The quince that we know in this country has to be cooked to be palatable, but the varieties that grow in tropical and sub-tropical climates can be eaten raw.

The Romans made a dish called *melomeli*, which entailed sealing ripe quince, covered with honey, in a wide-necked flagon and leaving them to mature. The dish was served at wedding feasts as a symbol of love.

THE MULBERRY tree was a common sight in Elizabethan gardens. It grows to a great age and size and the branches often need propping up with wooden stakes. In the gardens of Syon House, Brentford, stands a mulberry tree that is said to have been planted by the botanist, Turner, in 1584.

The Black mulberry, which was introduced to this country from Asia, is the species that produces edible fruits. The White mulberry is a native of China, brought to England in the 17th century as food for silkworms.

Mulberries are full of seeds but they have a very individual and captivating flavour. They make delicious jams, ice-creams, sorbets and summer puddings.

FLOWER SEEDS.

Sweet Pea.

It was once believed that the mulberry and quince should be grown together as husband and wife. That way the family who owned the land upon which they stood would prosper.

BLACKBERRIES have been harvested for many thousands of years. Archaeologists have found blackberry pips in the stomach of a neolithic man. Today town dwellers and country folk alike take pleasure in gathering this wild harvest to make jams, jellies, pies, tarts and drinks. Wild blackberries are definitely more flavoursome than the garden varieties which have been developed for the eye and ease of picking rather than the palate.

And sloes dim-covered as with dewy veils
And rambling bramble berries pulp and sweet
Arching their prickly trails
Half o'er the narrow lane.

JOHN CLARE

The weather of October is usually distinguished by its variability, heavy rains, high winds and sharp frosts . . . There is generally a sharp frost about the 12th, and anything likely to be injured . . . should be under shelter by the end of the first week.

THE GARDEN ORACLE, 1896

DIG AND FERTILIZE

Now is the time to dig over and fertilize flower beds and vegetable plots. Vacant plots should also be dug and left rough, to enable the weather to work upon the soil.

NETTLES were once thought to have magical powers because early farmers noticed that other plants grew well in their vicinity. In fact they store chemicals like nitrogen, phosphate, protein, silica and minerals such as iron.

This recipe for nettle fertilizer dates from the 16th century:

Cut nettles just before they flower and put them into a wooden cask. Fill with rainwater and leave to ferment for one month. Dilute with ten parts of rainwater and spray onto freshly dug ground.

SOOT is rich in nitrogen in the form of ammonium salts. It darkens the soil and, in cold weather allows the soil to absorb more heat from what little sun there is. You should let soot weather in a pile for at least six months before using.

The cure for this ill, is not to sit still,
Or frowst with a book by the fire;
But to take a large hoe and a shovel also,
And dig till you gently perspire.

RUDYARD KIPLING

THE VEGETABLE GARDEN

BRUSSELS SPROUTS are still a popular vegetable choice in Belgium today. It is not known when they were introduced to this country, but what is certain is that along with cabbage, they suffer from some of the worst cooking that England can produce. To cook sprouts correctly, they should be freshly picked and dropped into rapidly boiling, salted water for 5-10 minutes, depending on their size. When still firm to the bite, they should be drained and returned to a pan containing melted butter. Sauté the sprouts for 5 minutes or so and turn into a hot serving dish.

Brussels sprouts benefit from a little frost action and should be eaten after the first frosts, but before they become overgrown and frost-blighted.

Spray sprouts and cabbages with methylated spirits to protect them from mildew.

TURNIPS and SWEDES are part of the cabbage family, and subject to the same range of pests and diseases. Turnips were used in Tudor times as a cure for coughs and consumption. A remedial dish was made with layers of sliced turnip sprinkled with brown sugar and baked in the oven. Perhaps more to the modern taste would be a dish of glazed young turnips, cooked until just tender, drained of all but 2 tablespoons of the cooking water and then caramelised with 2 teaspoons of sugar and a good knob of butter and cooked until golden brown.

If, while working in the garden, your rake falls prong upwards, there will be heavy rain next day.

Sutton's Amateur's Guide in

For full info
see Enlarged
with Seeds.

Sutton's

pale gr
delicio
variet

BRUSSELS
SPROUTS.
(See accompany-
ing reports.)

SUTTON'S
EXHIBITION
Per ounce, 1s.

tton's Matchless.

𝓛UCKY STONES

Stones were once believed to grow from a mother stone whilst lying in the earth. A stone with a hole in its centre was said to be lucky for its finder. White glassy stones which are sometimes turned over in the garden were known as 'god-stones' and were thought to bring wealth and prosperity to the gardener.

𝓣HE HERB GARDEN

CARAWAY has been widely used for centuries and many superstitions have grown around its use. It was believed to keep things in their place – to prevent the theft of objects that contained it, to prevent a thief from leaving a house in which it was present, to keep lovers together and to keep homing pigeons at home. In Germany, a dish of caraway seeds would be placed under a child's crib to guard against witchcraft, and in ancient Egypt the dead were buried with it.

Queen Victoria's maids were fond of chewing caraway seeds. They were said to sweeten the breath and, according to Culpeper, the seeds were excellent for moving flatulence and helping with kidney disorders. A confection of caraway seeds dipped in sugar and taken a spoonful at a time was considered very beneficial to the digestion. The roots of the caraway can be boiled as a vegetable and the young leaves used in soups.

CORIANDER is one of the bitter herbs eaten by the Jews at the time of the Passover. It is mentioned in the Bible and was introduced into Britain by the Romans, when its principle use was as a preservative for meat. In the Middle Ages, coriander was considered an aphrodisiac, the warmth of its spice was thought to heat the blood. Today this herb is more associated with Indian than English cookery.

Victorian children were given little comfits, or sweets, made from sugar-coated coriander seeds. This may have been rather dangerous, as consumed in great numbers these seeds have narcotic properties.

Coriander was an ingredient in the liqueur eau-de-Carne, which was made in Paris in the 17th century. This was apparently used both as a perfume and a drink. The herb has also been used to flavour gin.

$\mathscr{T}$REES

Trees are prominent and permanent landmarks in the garden, they determine the scale and the living conditions for the plants and shrubs that surround them. Of course to the country-dweller, trees have a language all their own.

THE ELDER was thought to be the tree from which Judas Iscariot hanged himself, and it is therefore considered very unlucky to bring elder wood into the house and very foolish to burn it. Farmers would not use it to make sticks to drive their cattle, and to beat a child with an elder stick was thought to stunt its growth.

> '$\mathscr{W}$hen an oake is felling, it gives a kind of shrieke of groanes that may be heard a mile off, as if it were the genius of the oake lamenting.'
>
> AUBREY, *NATURAL HISTORY OF WILTSHIRE*

> $\mathscr{B}$eware the oak,
> it draws the stroke
> Avoid the ash,
> it courts the flash
> Creep under a thorn,
> it will keep you from harm.
>
> (ADVICE ON CHOOSING SHELTER IN A THUNDERSTORM)

THE HORSE-CHESTNUT has been loved by children for generations, as it gives them 'conkers' to play with. Its name 'horse' means 'coarse' or 'rough', although one popular belief is that its name comes from the curious markings on its smaller branches which resemble minute horse's hooves, perfect in every detail down to the seven nail marks.

THE OAK has been considered a holy tree in almost every country where it is native. It was actually worshipped by the Druids and the Celts who thought it not just unlucky to damage an oak, but actually sinful. The Romans dedicated the oak to Jupiter, lord of the gods and the god of rain and thunder.

NOVEMBER

The fogs and excess of atmospheric humidity render this the most cheerless month of the year, and therefore every effort should be made to maintain the conservatory and other structures devoted to ornamental plants.

THE GARDEN ORACLE, 1896

Cut chrysanthemums will last longer if you dip the cut ends into very hot water and then immediately into very cold water.

THE FLOWER GARDEN
Chrysanthemum

THIS IS AN ENORMOUS FAMILY OF PLANTS, ranging from simple daisies to monstrous blooms grown specifically for flower shows. Chrysanthemums were written of by Confucius as early as 500BC. They were flowers much loved by the Chinese nobility and in that country they are a sign of rest and ease. To English Victorian ladies they were a symbol of cheerfulness and optimism.

One old variety that originates from Persia is known as the Insect Powder Plant and it produces a remarkably useful dust that is lethal to small insects yet harmless to humans.

THE PENTSTEMON comes from Mexico and was introduced into this country in 1828. It is easy to grow and very attractive, and will provide colour in the border well into November in sheltered districts. Many varieties can still be obtained which date from the mid-19th century.

Bonfires

The garden needs to be tidied up in November. Garden rubbish not needed for compost should be heaped up and burned in a continuation of the custom of lighting bonfires at the beginning of November to mark the winter solstice. In the time of the Druids these bonfires would have included human sacrifice to encourage the sun's return and the continued fertility of the soil.

Ash from the bonfire should be collected while still dry and sprinkled around fruit trees. This will supply the trees with potash which is especially beneficial if the trees are growing in grass. The amount of potash varies according to the wood being burned. Bracken, tree prunings and pea and bean stalks provide the richest supply.

Wood for Burning

Beechwood fires burn bright and clear
If the logs are kept a year:
Chestnuts only good they say
If for years 'tis stored away:
Birch and firwood burn too fast,
Blaze too bright and do not last.
But ashwood green and ashwood brown,
Are fit for a Queen with a golden crown.

Oaken logs, if dry and old
Keep away the winter's cold:
Poplar gives a bitter smoke,
Fills you eyes and makes you choke:
Elmwood burns like churchyard mould,
Even the very flames are cold:
Applewood will scent the room:
Pearwood smells like flowers in bloom:
But ashwood wet and ashwood dry,
A King may warm his slippers by.

ANON

A NOVEMBER CALENDAR

1st November
ALL SAINT'S DAY

The Christian Church decreed this a day of prayer for all the saints in paradise, and 'Soulers', as they were called, went from house to house begging for gifts in return for their prayers. The householder would obviously offer what he had in abundance. In November that usually meant apples and pears.

2nd November
ALL SOUL'S DAY

This is the day set aside by the church for praying for the souls in purgatory. In the 18th century fires of gorse were lit to lead the souls to paradise.

11th November
ST. MARTIN'S DAY

Ice before Martinmas enough to bear a duck.
The rest of the winter is sure to be a muck.

20th November
ST. EDMUND'S DAY

St. Edmund is the patron saint of farm and garden workers.

23rd November
ST. CLEMENT'S DAY

St Clement gives the winter

The direction of the wind at midnight on St Clement's Day forecast the conditions that will prevail until Candlemas, 2nd February.

25th November
ST. CATHERINE'S DAY

St. Catherine's foul or fair
So it will be next Februair.

Put your hand in your pocket
And pull out your keys,
Go down to the cellar,
And draw what you please.
Soul, soul, for an apple or two,
If you have no apples, pears will do.

SHROPSHIRE SOULING SONG

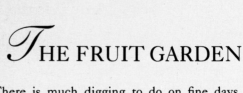

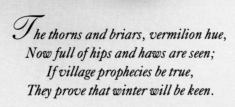

THE FRUIT GARDEN

There is much digging to do on fine days in November, particularly in the kitchen garden where the ground must be prepared for spring planting. Old-fashioned gardeners would guard against back-ache by carrying a conker in their pocket.

THE PEAR is thought to have originated in Southern Europe and Western Asia. The pear tree flowers in April and May with blossoms of pure white and the fruit, at first green, turns yellow as it ripens.

Old English varieties such as *Black Worcester* (which appears on the coat of arms of the City of Worcester) and *Catillac* can be stored in the same way as apples. These are hard, cooking pears and are best served stewed.

THE MEDLAR was a popular fruit in the 16th century. It resembles a very small russett apple with a thick skin that is rough and greenish brown. In some parts of the country it is known as 'openers' for its laxative qualities. The flowers appear in May and June and are very lovely. Medlars must be left to decay (blett) before they are fit to eat. The fruit must be gathered when it is on the point of falling, then it must be stored in tissue paper or straw until over-ripe. It can then be roasted with butter and cloves or made into a jelly.

The thorns and briars, vermilion hue,
Now full of hips and haws are seen;
If village prophecies be true,
They prove that winter will be keen.

JOHN CLARE

The Medlar tree attracts honey
bees by the score.

Two pear trees are better than
one as most varieties need a
partner for pollination.

THE VEGETABLE GARDEN

THE POTATO was cultivated as long ago as 750 BC by the Peruvians. Sir Francis Drake brought the potato from Virginia in North America to England in 1585. According to physicians and herbalists, the potato was a powerful aphrodisiac – a conclusion reached in respect of every newly-introduced species! It was, at one time, widely believed to be poisonous and therefore had no place in the kitchen. This may have been because people had tried eating the green potato tops which are both poisonous and unappetising.

When the English finally understood the potato, it was grown as a delicacy for the tables of the rich, but as their valuable food properties became known, the Royal Society encouraged their cultivation for the masses in case of famine.

Now there is an enormous variety of potatoes available, from the oblong and waxy (best for salads) to the round and mealy (best for mashing). It is said that to carry a piece of raw potato in the pocket will ease the pain of rheumatism.

THE LEEK is a member of the Liliaceae (lily) family. It is a hardy plant and will withstand winter frosts. It was used in the 16th century as a cure for drunkenness and the stewed vegetable was used as a poultice in cases of snake bite and piles.

Properly cooked, it is among the most delicious of all vegetables. As an alternative to boiled or braised leeks, try sautéeing raw leek, cut into strips, with a generous handful of diced streaky bacon.

Leeks planted close to carrots will repel carrot fly.

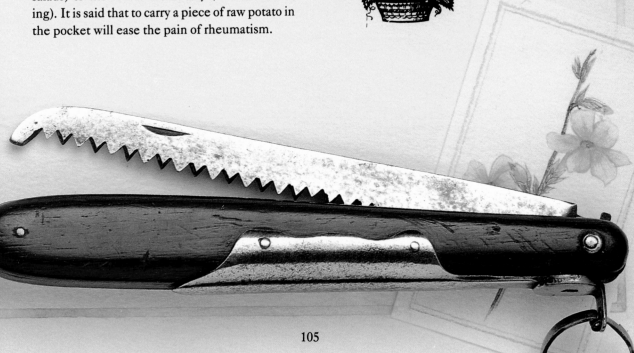

December

Silly gardener! Summer goes
And winter comes with pinching toes,
When in the garden bare and brown
You must lay your barrow down!

R. L. STEVENSON

How like a winter hath my absence been
From thee, the pleasure of the fleeting year!
What freezings have I felt, what dark days seen!
What old December's bareness everywhere!

W. SHAKESPEARE

Ivy will thrive on the grave of
any young girl who died for love.

THE WINTER GARDEN
Holly and Ivy

THE EVERGREEN HOLLY is a slow-growing tree that will stand almost all conditions of soil and climate. Legend has it that the cross was made of holly wood and for that reason the holly must suffer by bearing thorny leaves. Its berries are supposed to represent drops of Christ's blood – before the crucifixion it was thought that all holly berries were yellow.

The number of berries is said to foretell winter weather: few berries means a mild winter as the birds will be able to find food from many sources; an abundance of berries means extra provisions for the birds in view of harsh conditions to follow.

The holly tree represents masculinity, steadfastness and holiness and is used as a decoration at Christmas to presage the forthcoming sadness of Good Friday.

IVY was known to the Greeks as *Cissos* after a young dancing girl who collapsed and died of exhaustion at the feet of Dionysus after dancing before the gods at a feast. So moved was he that he turned her body into ivy, which embraces anything it touches. Because of its clinging properties, ivy is seen as the female counterpart of the masculine holly and, needless to say, as a symbol of unpredictability.

Ivy is credited with the power to prevent drunkenness.

MISTLETOE is an ancient symbol of fertility that was used by the Druids in their rituals. On the sixth night of the moon, so it is said, white-robed Druids would cut mistletoe from their sacred oaks with golden sickles. It was not allowed to fall to the ground, but caught in a white cloth, for the Druids believed that mistletoe contained the life of the oak tree – a very potent magic. In Greek mythology, the golden bough which Aeneas plucked from the oak at the gate of the underworld as a token of safe conduct was thought to be a branch of mistletoe.

The custom of kissing under the mistletoe is a relic of the ancient belief in the powers of its berries. A man was said to be able to assert his supremacy with this plant, demanding a kiss for every berry in the kissing bough.

In Staffordshire, farmer's wives would keep a bunch of mistletoe from one Christmas till the next to burn on the fire under the Christmas pudding.

THE CHRISTMAS ROSE is thought to be one of the oldest cultivated plants. Known as the black hellebore – meaning injurious food in Greek – it is a poisonous plant. It was reputed to have been used by physicians to cure a princess of Argos of a severe mental affliction and, according to early herbalists, it was still being used (in very small quantities) to cure madness in the 16th and 17th centuries.

For all its poison, it is a very pretty plant with smooth shiny leaves and pure white blossoms that obligingly blooms in the very depths of winter.

*Borage and Hellebore fill two scenes
Sovereign plants to purge the veins
Of melancholy, and cheer the heart
Of those black fumes which make it smart.*

ROBERT BURTON

CHRISTMAS GIFTS

A few drops of brandy will revive a pot-pourri that has lost its fragrance.

How to make
A CHRISTMAS POT-POURRI

2oz/50g dried orange peel
2oz/50g dried lemon peel
$\frac{1}{2}$oz/15g whole allspice berries
1oz/25g lightly crushed cinnamon sticks
1oz/25g star anise
1oz/25g dried pine needles
$\frac{1}{2}$oz/15g whole cloves
2oz/50g dried rowan berries
1oz/25g small larch cones
$\frac{1}{2}$oz/15g dried applemint leaves
$\frac{1}{2}$oz/15g dried sage leaves
1oz/25g dried powdered orris root
1oz/25g sandalwood raspings

Mix all the ingredients together and put into a large bowl in the hall or by the front door to welcome guests over the Christmas period.

How to make
A POMANDER BALL

Press cloves into the skin of a perfect thin skinned orange. Either cover the whole orange with cloves, allowing a little space between each one for shrinkage as the orange dries, or set them in patterns around the orange. Roll the finished orange in a mixture of orris root and spices – cinnamon or allspice. Tie a ribbon round to suspend the pomander, which should hold its scent for a year or more.

A DECEMBER CALENDAR

21st December
ST. THOMAS'S DAY

This day, being the shortest and the turning point of the year, has been an important festival since time immemorial. The festivities were linked to the fertility of the soil and the longed-for return of the sun.

Many traditions grew up regarding the planting of seeds at this time of the year. In the south-east of England, broad beans would be planted on this day and the wise gardener would check the skin of his onions on St. Thomas' Day to ascertain the weather for the coming winter months.

Onion skins very thin
Mild winter coming in.
Onion skins thick and tough
Coming winter very rough.

COTSWOLD SAYING

14th-28th December
HALCYON DAYS

The seven days before and the seven days after St. Thomas's Day were known as the Halcyon Days. The old name for the kingfisher was halcyon, and it was thought that at this time the gods granted a respite from winter storms to this lovely bird to enable her to hatch her young in peace.

24th December
CHRISTMAS EVE

This is the day to take precautions to ensure a good crop of fruit. On Christmas Eve, straw should be bound around the trunks of all fruit trees. Fruit props cut on this day when the sap is low will, so it is said, last forever.

Girls who wish to see an image of their future partner should take this opportunity to walk backwards around the nearest pear tree nine times.

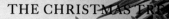

THE CHRISTMAS TREE

There is a long tradition of taking greenery into the house at this time of the year. In Egyptian times, branches of palm were used to celebrate the winter solstice and the Romans used evergreen branches in their celebration of Saturnalia when sacrifices were offered to protect winter-sown crops.

The Christmas tree tradition, as we know it, comes from Germany, and Prince Albert is credited with importing the idea into Britain. There is a charming, though most unlikely story associated with the origin of this particular custom. The Christ Child is said to have appeared to a poor peasant family one cold winter's night. The child looked so hungry and thin that the forester took pity on him and fed and cared for him. When the family awoke next morning, the cottage was bathed in heavenly light and sweet music played. As the child left, he pulled a branch from a nearby fir tree and stuck it in the ground, saying that it would provide food and comfort each winter in repayment of the family's kindness.

However, its real origin lies in the rites associated with the Scandinavian Tree of Time, which itself is derived from winter solstice symbols of everlasting life and mystic fertility, as was its summer counterpart, the maypole. Decorating the tree with lights is said to have originated in the Jewish Festival of Hanukkah – the Festival of Light.

The variety of fir most commonly used as a Christmas tree is the Norwegian Spruce. If you buy one with its roots still intact and water it well, it should not shed its needles and you will be able to plant it out in the garden when the festivities are over.

And now fir tree . . .
Acclaimed by eager, blue-eyed girls and boys,
Bursts into tinsel, fruit and glittering toys
And turns into a pyramid of light.

EUGENE LEE HAMILTON

JANUARY

Cold is the winter day, misty and dark;
The sunless sky with faded gleams is rent:
And patches of thick snow outlying mark
The landscape with drear disfigurement.

ROBERT BRIDGES

Brother, Joy to you
I've brought some snowdrops; only just a few,
But quite enough to prove the world awake,
Cheerful and hopeful in the frosty dew
And for the pale sun's sake.

CHRISTINA ROSETTI

Grass that grows in Janiveer
Grows no more all the year

THE WINTER GARDEN

Snowdrop

A MEMBER OF THE DAFFODIL FAMILY, the snowdrop is a native of the alpine areas of Europe and Asia. It has long been considered a sacred plant, a holy symbol of chastity and purity. It is also a symbol of death, and in many areas of England it was considered bad luck to carry a single bloom into the house. The Victorians considered it a death token, likening the outer petals to a shroud and reading into the fact that the blossoms grow close to the bare earth, a sure sign that this beautiful flower belonged more to the dead than to the living.

VIRBURNUM FRAGRENS is one of the few evergreen plants to bloom in the January garden. It is a native of northern China and it produces fragrant white flowers from November through to February.

A JANUARY CALENDAR

1st January
ST. FAINE'S DAY
Whether the weather be snow or rain
We are sure to see the flower of St. Faine.
Rain comes but seldom and often snow
And yet the Viburnum is sure to blow.

5th-6th January
TWELFTH NIGHT
On Twelfth night, in many areas it was common practice to wassail apple trees. In order to wish the tree and its spirit good health, or *waes heil*, revellers would gather around a large old apple tree and consume a great deal of cider and sing their toasts to the gods who dwelt in the orchards.

It is also the time to take down Christmas decorations as it is considered extremely unlucky to leave them up after Twelfth Night. Care must be taken with evergreen boughs, they must never be discarded but rather ceremoniously burnt or buried with due reverence in the garden.

13th January
ST. HILARY'S DAY
Wrap up warm and protect susceptible plants from frost – this is supposed to be the coldest day of the year.

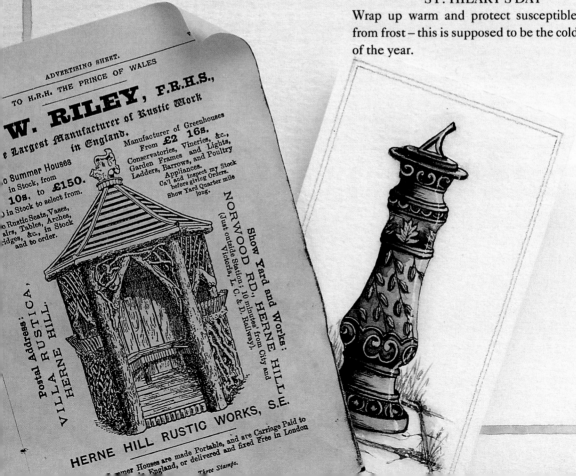

22nd January
ST. VINCENT'S DAY
Remember on St. Vincent's Day
If that the sun his beams display
For 'tis a token, bright and clear,
Of prosperous weather all the year.

25th January
ST. PAUL'S DAY
In the 16th and 17th centuries the nation was
called upon to pray for a bright, sunny day. A dull
day was supposedly an omen of war and disaster.

FEEDING BIRDS IN WINTER

Each species of garden bird likes a different kind
of food, so the more varied a menu you can offer,
the more bird species you will attract.

Magpies, starlings, tits and crows like scraps
of meat and fat, such as bacon rind. Commercial
seed mixtures will attract finches, while fruit –
preferably apples – is popular with blackbirds
and thrushes. Robins are partial to mealworms,
which you can buy as angling bait, and with a
little patience you can get these most engaging
of garden birds to eat out of your hand.

If Janiver's calends be summerly gay
Twill be wintery weather to the calends of May.

Here's to thee, old apple tree!
Whence thou may'st bud and whence thou may'st blow
And whence thou may'st have apples enow!

If in January, the sun much appear
March and April pay full dear.

TWELFTH NIGHT WASSAILING SONG

THE SYMBOLISM OF TREES

This is the month to cut down any dangerous, diseased or old trees. However, before felling a tree it is a wise precaution to ask its permission. This will placate the tree spirits who might otherwise cause some dreadful accident to occur.

THE WILLOW is a symbol of grief and those who have been forsaken in love. Deserted lovers would 'wear the green willow' to share their heartache with the world. Willow catkins are lovely – some of the varieties of shrubby willows sport clusters of silvery catkins which turn to gold as the pollen appears. It is said, however, that willow catkins should not be brought indoors as they will bring bad luck.

THE ASH, like many trees, was believed to be a protector against evil. To find an ash leaf with an equal number of divisions on each side was considered extremely fortunate. It should be picked and the following rhyme repeated:

> Even ash, I do thee pluck,
> Hoping thus to meet good luck
> If no good luck I get from thee,
> I shall wish thee on the tree.

The finder should wear the leaf in his hat or carry it in his pocket and he can expect to find success and happiness, or at worst, protection from mishaps.

The even ash leaf was used as a love charm in some parts of the country. The following rhyme is from Northumberland:

> Even, even ash
> I pluck thee off the tree
> The first young man that I do meet
> My lover he shall be.

THE ASPEN AND THE POPLAR are both referred to as the 'shiver tree' because the leaves of both trees tremble with any air movements. This has led to the belief that they would cure fever and tremblings. One method of affecting a cure was to pin a lock of your hair to the tree and recite the following:

> Aspen tree, aspen tree,
> I prithee shake and shiver instead of me.

In the case of the poplar the rhyme goes:

> Poplar, when Christ Our Lord was on the cross,
> Then did'st thou shiver and toss.
> My aches and pains thou now must take,
> Instead of me I bid thee shake.

Willow whiten, aspens quiver,
Little breezes dusk and shiver

ALFRED, LORD TENNYSON

The poor soul sat sighing by a sycamore tree,
Sing all a green willow;
Her hand on her bosom, her head on her knee,
Sing willow, willow, willow:
The fresh streams ran by her, and murmured her moans;
Sing willow, willow, willow;
Her salt tears fell from her and soften'd the stones.
Sing willow, willow, willow.

W. SHAKESPEARE

FEBRUARY

But now 'tis winter, child,
And bitter northwinds blow,
The ways are wet and wild
The land is laid with snow

ROBERT BRIDGES

If Candlemas Day be fair and bright
Winter will have another flight;
If on Candlemas Day it be shower and rain,
Winter is gone and will not come again.

Much February snow
A fine summer doth show.

THE WINTER GARDEN

Primrose

ALWAYS A WELCOME SIGHT in this otherwise bleak month, the primrose was, for many centuries, considered to be a magical flower. The primrose is one of the earliest of spring flowers. In rural England they are known as fairy cups, as it was widely believed that the fairies dwelt within the yellow flowers, using them for shelter in rainstorms.

Herbalists recommend adding primrose leaves to a salad to cure arthritis and an ointment of these leaves was said to be soothing for burns and ulcers. The primrose was once held in high esteem as a beauty treatment – it was said to add to beauty or restore its loss. Country girls used primrose leaves to rub on their cheeks to cause a pink blush, much as they might use rouge today.

In the kitchen, the primrose can be used to flavour custards and as a basis for a delicious country wine. A word of warning, though, primroses growing wild must not be picked as they are now a protected species. If you wish to try any old primrose recipes, then you should grow your own from seed.

Contrary to general opinion, February is the driest month of the year, and, when the weather is not exceptionally severe, affords a favourable opportunity for pushing on outdoor work of all descriptions.

THE GARDEN ORACLE, 1896

A FEBRUARY CALENDAR

2nd February
CANDLEMAS

Candlemas is the familiar name for the Feast of the Purification of the Virgin Mary and the Presentation of Christ in the Temple. Before the Reformation, Christians in Britain lit candles on this day to signify that Christ was the Light of the World. Special services were held and the candles were blessed and taken home by members of the congregation to light the windows of their houses and cottages.

It is said to be the day the hedgehog leaves its winter hibernation to look at the weather.

14th February
ST. VALENTINE'S DAY

The celebration of love that is associated with this day probably has little to do with the obscure St. Valentine. It is more likely to have derived from the Roman festival of Lupercalia, a celebration of fertility that was held in mid-February.

According to folklore, this was the day on which birds chose their mates, and this is probably the origin of the sending of love tokens and messages in the name of St. Valentine.

24th February
ST. MATTHIAS'S DAY

On this day it was believed that the trees threw off their winter sleep. As the great trees began to stir themselves, the cottagers could look forward to the beginning of spring and the promise of better days ahead.

> St. Mathee sends
> The sap up the trees!

THE PANSY is a flower particularly associated with St. Valentine's Day. It is the emblem of love and kind thoughts, hence its common name of hearts-ease. Other country names for the pansy are love-in-idleness, kiss-her-in-the-pantry and tickle-my-fancy. An infusion of pansy leaves is said to cure a broken heart, and it was the juice of the pansy of which Shakespeare wrote in *A Midsummer Night's Dream*:

> The juice of it, on sleeping eyelids laid,
> Will make a man or woman madly dote
Upon the next live creature that it sees.

But a final word of warning: to pick a pansy flower with the dew upon it, will result in the death of a loved one.

> *T*he hedgehog hides beneath the rotten hedge
> And makes a great round nest of grass and sedge
> Or in a bush or in a hollow tree
> And many often stoop and say they see
> Him roll and fill his prickles full of crabs
> And creep away . . .

JOHN CLARE

THE FORGET-ME-NOT is also associated with St. Valentine's Day. It is a flower which can be found in most parts of the world. This was said to be because an angel once fell in love with a mortal woman and was banished from heaven. He could only return if he placed forget-me-nots in every corner of the globe. The angel and his lover travelled tirelessly planting these little flowers. So hard did they work that St. Peter took pity on them and allowed them both into heaven. In the Language of Flowers, the forget-me-not means friendship and fidelity, as well as remembrance.

How to make
A PRESSED FLOWER PICTURE

Flowers for pressing should be picked in their prime. Since the colours tend to fade, it is worth selecting flowers that come in bright colours like poppies, violets and daffodils.

Once the flowers are picked they have to be dissected. Multi-petalled ones should be taken apart completely, a daffodil works well if sliced in half and violets and pansies are simple enough to use whole. All flowers should be separated from their stems and leaves as you will find that the original stems rarely have the right curve or flow for pressing, so it is advisable to pick several flowers purely for their stems and leaves.

Place the dissected flowers between two pieces of blotting paper and put the blotting paper inside a heavy book or flower press and leave for at least three months.

To assemble your picture, first lay the stems and petals out on your chosen piece of card to define the design, then stick them into place with a transparent glue sparingly applied to the card, not the flower.

THE SYMBOLISM OF HERBS

THE BAY TREE is believed to be a healer and a protector. In the ancient world it was a symbol of victory and honour. Letters announcing victory were wrapped in bay leaves and heroes were crowned with them. In Christian times it was seen as a symbol of the resurrection because of its ability to revive when apparently quite dead.

It was believed that bay trees were never struck by lightning and planted near a house they would protect it from all kinds of evil. The leaves were also used for divination – if a handful thrown into the fire crackled noisily as they burnt it was a good omen, if they burnt silently the omen was bad. And it is said the sudden withering of bay leaves foretells pestilence or the death of kings.

'Tis thought the king is dead;
we will not stay.
The bay trees in our country
are all wither'd.

W. SHAKESPEARE

Better is a dinner of herbs
where love is, than a stalled ox
and hatred therewith.

THE BIBLE *PROVERBS*

BALM is used by beekeepers to attract stray swarms to their hives as it is a plant particularly attractive to bees. In the past balm was taken to relieve melancholy. Today its delicious lemon-scented leaves are used to good advantage in long, cool drinks.

Balm is sovereign for the brain, strengthening the memory and powerfully chasing away melancholy.

JOHN EVELYN

SAGE has a long history as a medicinal herb. Its Latin name *salvia* comes from the word *salvere* meaning to be healthy. There are many tales told about sage: it was believed that if a man grew sage in his garden he would never die; that as long as his sage bush was healthy, his business would prosper; that it could assuage grief and that when sage grows vigorously in the garden, the wife rules the house.

In Culpeper's Herbal there is a long list of ailments for which sage is a remedy. They range from pains in the head, rheumatism and hoarseness through to greying hair, discoloured teeth and failing memory.

Grow mint in the garden to attract money to your purse.

If the sage bush thrives and grows, The master's not master – And he knows!

MINT was thought of as a cure-all by 17th century herbalists who used it in remedies for everything from colic to venereal disease. It was one of the sweet herbs loved by the Elizabethans who used it to strew around the floors of their chambers. The leaves are at their most aromatic before the flowers appear.

INDEX

BIBLIOGRAPHY

Garden Flower Folklore, Laura C. Martin, Globe Pequot Press

The Compleat Strawberry, Stafford Whiteaker, Century Publishing Co. Ltd.

The Concise British Flora in Colour, W. Keble Martin, Sphere Books

Gardener's Delight, John Seymour, Dorling, Kindersley

Gardening for Gourmets, Ray Procter, Thomas Nelson & Sons Ltd.

Home-made Country Wines, compiled by Dorothy Wise, Hamlyn

The Penguin Book of Herbs and Spices, Rosemary Hemphill

Back to the Roots, Richard Mabey and Francesca Greenoak, Arrow Books Ltd.

The Customs and Ceremonies of Britain, Charles Kightly, Thames and Hudson

Old Wives' Lore for Gardeners, Maureen and Bridget Boland, Futura Publications

British Calendar Customs, Wright & Lones, The Folklore Society, 1936

The National Trust Guide to Traditional Customs of Britain, Brian Shuel, Webb and Bower

Dictionary of Christian Lore and Legend, J.C.J. Metford, Thames and Hudson

ACKNOWLEDGEMENTS

DORLING KINDERSLEY would like to thank the following people for help with photography:
Sutton Seeds Ltd, Torquay for the loan of seed catalogues; Roy Arnold, Needham Market for the loan of gardening equipment; St Paul's Church, Bedford Street, London WC2 for help with flowers.

And the following for the loan of photographs:
Nicholas Hall, p19; Institute of Agricultural History and Museum of Rural Life, University of Reading, p25, 27, 28, 30, 33, 46, 55, 73, 83; Stephen Bull, pp43, 57, 91; F. E. Bull, pp48–49; Mrs G. F. Bull, p56; BBC Hulton Picture Library, p68; Jane Mathewson Bull, p73; Beamish North of England Open Air Museum, p79; Somerset County Museums Service Photographic Library, p86; Luton Museum and Art Gallery, p96; Ian Jacob, p99

Dorling Kindersley would also like to thank, Alex Parsons for her help on the manuscript, Catherine Treasure for additional research and Rebecca Jack for picture research.

AUTHOR'S ACKNOWLEDGEMENTS

Judy and Ben Green for verification of many gardening facts; Julia Dixon for the loan of her wonderful book 'The Garden Oracle'; Judi Lang for information patiently relayed over the phone, and also to the following for their interest and help during the writing of this book, Vera Knight and Margaret Smith, John and Joan Tann of Crapes Fruit Farm in Essex, Paul Shaddock, ESDC and also the staff of the relevant departments of the public and reference libraries in the City of Birmingham. Paul Shaddock, ESDC.